*Nursing and midwifery in the poor-law unions of Borrisokane and Nenagh,
1882–1922*

Maynooth Studies in Local History

SERIES EDITOR Michael Potterton

This is one of six volumes in the Maynooth Studies in Local History series for 2022. It is also my first year as series editor, having taken over the role from the irreplaceable Raymond Gillespie, who held that position from 1995 to 2021, overseeing the publication of a veritable treasure trove of studies in those 27 years. Raymond established the series with Irish Academic Press as a direct result of the enormous success of the Maynooth MA in Local History programme, which began in 1992. Under Raymond's supervision, some 153 volumes were produced, authored by 140 different scholars (94 men and 46 women). The first volume, on education in nineteenth-century Meath, was written by Paul Connell, and the 153rd, on the Dublin Cattle Market in the 1950s and 1960s, was by Declan O'Brien. Eleven people have each contributed two volumes to the series, while Terry Dooley is the only person to have written three.

The remarkable collection now covers some 1,500 years of history across 31 counties, dealing variously with aspects of agriculture and fishing, architecture, crime and punishment, death and burial, economy and trade, education, famine, gender, healthcare, industry, language and literature, migration, music and the arts, politics, religion, society, travel and communication, urban development, war and much more besides. I am grateful to Raymond for entrusting the series to me, and to Four Courts Press for not vetoing the appointment. Together, I am sure that we can build on the sound foundations established over more than quarter of a century of diligent work.

The current crop of titles takes us from a broad look at religion and society in medieval Galway to a very specific and tragic event in Knockcroghery village on the night of 20 June 1921. En route we witness the gradual dismantling of Irish lordship in early modern north Co. Cork, and the development of nursing and midwifery in Co. Tipperary at the turn of the twentieth century. Finally, we have biographical sketches of two remarkable men of the nineteenth century – Thomas Conolly (1823–76) of Castletown House in Co. Kildare and botanist Nathaniel Colgan (1851–1919) of Dublin.

While the genesis and home of this series lie firmly at Maynooth, it is a mark of its appeal, its breadth and its inclusivity that this year's contributors are drawn from Carlow College, Glenstal Abbey, NUI Galway, Trinity College Dublin and the University of Limerick as well as Maynooth University.

Maynooth Studies in Local History: Number 157

Nursing and midwifery in the poor-law unions of Borrisokane and Nenagh, 1882–1922

Lisa Jane McGeeney

FOUR COURTS PRESS

Set in 11.5pt on 13.5pt Bembo by
Carrigboy Typesetting Services for
FOUR COURTS PRESS LTD
7 Malpas Street, Dublin 8, Ireland
www.fourcourtspress.ie
and in North America for
FOUR COURTS PRESS
c/o IPG, 814 N Franklin Street, Chicago, IL 60610

ISBN 978–1–80151–032–5

Printed in Ireland
by SprintPrint, Dublin

Contents

Acknowledgments

This work is based on research conducted for an MA in Local History at University of Limerick from 2018 to 2020 under the supervision of course director Dr David Fleming and Dr Coleman Dennehy. I wish to express my sincere gratitude to Dr Fleming whose guidance and support as both lecturer and supervisor have been consistently constructive, considered and encouraging. I also extend my gratitude to Dr Dennehy, as co-supervisor, for helping to clarify my ideas before I started writing and to each of my lecturers from both Mary Immaculate College and University of Limerick.

Every journey starts with the first step and for me that was the Certificate in Local History, which I completed in the Irish Workhouse Centre, Portumna, in 2018. I wish to thank all who developed and delivered this course: Steve Dolan, John Joe Conwell, Dr Christy Cunniffe, Clare Lowery, Ann O'Riordan and Zena Hoctor.

Thank you to the librarians and archivists in Glucksman Library, National Library of Ireland, Tipperary Studies in Thurles and Nenagh Library for their assistance in sourcing the books and documents I requested. Thank you to Nenagh historians Donal and Nancy Murphy for sharing valuable resources and documents as well as their own writings, which were used in this thesis. Thank you to Annette Delahunt whose stories of her grandmother, Mary Aherne, inspired me and for verifying my research on her great grandmother Helen Kelly. Thank you to Kilbarron Terryglass Historical Society for their continued interest in and support of my research, especially to Helen Fox for information on Julia Hough.

Thank you to my family, friends and colleagues who have supported me, especially my parents Mary and Michael and my husband Joe.

Introduction

From the 1880s health provision in Ireland was transformed with the development of nursing as a profession for women. Often poor and illiterate, nurses had been seen as occupying a low, servile position.[1] From the 1840s these perceptions began to change. English nursing reformers such as Elizabeth Fry and Florence Nightingale saw the need for formal training and sought to make nursing a noble profession for ladies to pursue; a mantle that would be taken up in Ireland by middle- and upper-class female philanthropists and female religious orders.[2] From the 1860s training schools for nurses were established in Dublin. These included the Adelaide Institution and Protestant Hospital, whose nursing school, established in 1861, was one of the first in Ireland (although it accepted only Protestants for training) and the Dublin Nurses Training Institution established in 1866 by Maria Trench and her husband Richard Chenevix Trench, the Protestant archbishop of Dublin.[3] Lectures in midwifery were available in the Rotunda Hospital, Dublin, for medical students and midwives from 1770 but it was only after the foundation of the Obstetrical Society in London in 1870 that midwives sat examinations and were awarded certificates of proficiency in midwifery.[4] The impact of this would be seen primarily in urban settings until the late nineteenth century when employment opportunities for qualified nurses and midwives opened up in rural areas. These positions were primarily in institutions such as the fever hospital, workhouse infirmary and dispensary system, or they established themselves as independent practitioners. Then, in the early twentieth century, the great public health crisis of tuberculosis would see the creation of new district nursing posts funded by the many branches of the Women's National Health Association, founded in 1907.[5] This work explores the emergence of the professional nurse in these public-health settings in the poor-law unions of Borrisokane and Nenagh, in north Tipperary, between 1882 and 1922. Chapter 1 identifies the number of nurses and midwives in these unions during the period as well as their social background and education.

Illness and poverty have always been so closely associated that many philanthropic institutions and societies founded in the eighteenth and nineteenth centuries had as their mission relief of the poor through providing medical assistance during times of illness.[6] The institutions established from the eighteenth century to meet the medical needs of the poor included the dispensary system, voluntary hospitals, county infirmaries, fever hospitals and lunatic asylums. These institutions were financed by grand-jury presentments, fines from petty sessions and voluntary subscriptions.[7] Most of these institutions were located in the major cities and towns, which meant that more rural places, such as Nenagh and Borrisokane, had no hospital provision. The county infirmary for Tipperary was established in 1768 in Cashel and the county asylum opened in Clonmel in 1835, both in south Tipperary, too far away to be a practical option for people in the north of the county.[8] They did, however, have access to the dispensary system established under an 1805 act of parliament to provide medical relief in those places with limited or no access to county hospitals.[9] There were also private physicians, surgeons, apothecaries, druggists, accoucheurs and ladies' nurse tenders available for those who could afford to engage their services but their numbers appear to have been small and many of the doctors, in particular, also worked in the public system.[10] Other healers, bonesetters and handywomen midwives were available but would not have been free of charge in money or kind, while the dispensary system was for those who were eligible. By 1835 there were dispensaries in Ballymackey, Borrisokane, Cloughjordan, Lorrha, Nenagh, Newport, Silvermines and Toomevara.[11] Those governing the country were conscious that if a labouring man fell ill and was unable to work and earn money to support his family, they quickly became destitute.[12] Preventing such a scenario formed much of the philosophy around providing medical relief to the poor.[13]

From 1829 the people of north Tipperary also had access to fever hospitals. Even before the development of germ theory as a cause of disease, the Irish people, from their experience of generations of endemic, fever-causing diseases, knew they were contagious, and that the best means of preventing their spread was to keep the sick separate from the well. Fever hospitals, for this purpose, began to be built in urban centres from 1807, with the development of district fever hospitals following the great fever epidemic of 1816–18.[14] These permanent structures were sometimes augmented by temporary fever hospitals such as during the cholera epidemic of 1832–3 when the boards of health ordered temporary cholera hospitals to be built in Nenagh, Lorrha, Borrisokane, Castletownarra (Portroe) and Cloughjordan.[15] There were three fever hospitals in Nenagh union prior to 1852, in Nenagh, Cloughjordan and Borrisokane. The first two were established by 1829 while Borrisokane was under construction at the time of the Poor Inquiry in 1835.[16] In 1847 Nenagh fever hospital was rebuilt with a seventy-bed capacity. Two years later, in 1849, the poor-law commissioners required the closure of Cloughjordan and Borrisokane fever hospitals, after which time all fever cases in the union would be sent to Nenagh.[17] The fever hospital in Borrisokane, located 1km from the main workhouse buildings, continued to be used at times when fever patients presented to the infirmary but it was often empty.[18]

The introduction of a new Irish poor law in 1838 saw the country divided into 163 unions of townlands and district electoral divisions by 1850 and the construction of a workhouse in each union, with infirmaries to care for those inmates who were sick.[19] This added another medical institution to the existing provision with subsequent legislation including the Medical Charities Act, 1851 and Poor Relief (Ireland) Act, 1862, which brought those services under the control of the poor laws and reorganized them.[20] These acts saw the workhouse hospitals becoming 'de facto district hospitals', with their services available to most people who required medical treatment, making these institutions the main form of public-health provision in many parts of Ireland until the poor laws were repealed by the Local Government (Temporary Provisions) Act, 1923 of the new Irish Free State.[21] Services provided under the poor laws were financed by a tax, the poor rate, based on the value of property as per the primary valuation of Ireland (Griffiths' valuation) carried out between 1848 and 1864, thereby eliminating the voluntary element of supporting the poor which had previously existed.[22]

The medical institutions that formed the system included both out-patient and in-patient services and comprised the dispensary system, fever hospitals and workhouse infirmaries.[23] This system, which provided free medical advice and treatment to paupers and the lower classes, was also available to others at a cost. It had its champions and its critics but it was those who sought improvements in both the care provided and the economy of operating the system who eventually brought about much-needed reforms.[24] During the seventy years in which it was the main source of health provision for the majority of the population, this system went through reforms and improvements. The changes pertinent to this book were related to the type and number of its nursing staff. It was a period in which increasing pressure was placed on boards of guardians to employ trained nurses to ensure higher standards of care for the sick, elderly and infirm.[25] In 1870, the Irish 'poor-law medical system' was pronounced by Dr Cameron, professor of hygiene to the Royal College of Surgeons, Ireland, to be the most perfect in the world, this being attributed to the hard work and skill of the dispensary physicians and to its being the most admirable sanitary organization in Europe.[26] In 1867, 788 poor-law medical officers and ninety-seven midwives in 718 dispensary districts with 1,042 dispensary stations attended 890,860 persons for sickness, representing about a sixth of the population.[27] It was not a perfect system, even if it was better than that available in other countries at that time. If it had been there would not have been so many calls for reform to aspects of the service. Improvements in care, cleanliness and management of the workhouse infirmaries emerged following the arrival of the Sisters of Mercy who, in 1861, took charge of Limerick union infirmary.[28] The success of this venture led to the nuns taking on this role in other unions.[29] In 1882 they arrived in Nenagh union infirmary and set about effecting similar reforms.[30] Further significant reforms were seen after 1896 as a result of the combined pressure from the newly formed Irish Workhouse Association and the Irish Medical Association, whose objectives included employing qualified nursing and midwifery staff and ceasing the use of 'pauper nurses'.[31] These inmates of the workhouse were allocated to work in the infirmary or fever hospital, in line with the rules of the workhouse, which required all able-bodied paupers to work for their keep, though they did not possess the necessary skills, aptitude or interest in caring for the sick.[32] The movement towards employing only qualified nurses in the workhouse infirmaries and fever hospitals would also impact the dispensary system where qualified midwives began to be employed in all dispensary areas and not just those with large populations.[33]

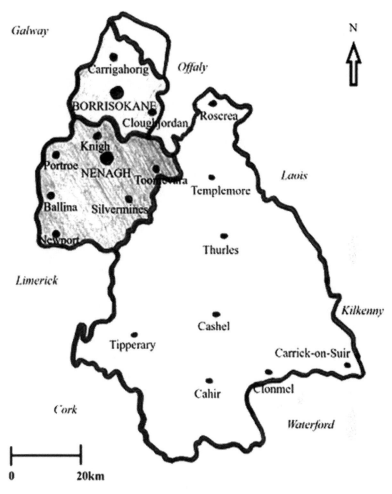

1. Map of Co. Tipperary with Borrisokane and Nenagh poor-law unions and major towns

Borrisokane poor-law union, which was established in 1850, was situated in the most northerly part of north Tipperary, with Nenagh poor-law union, established in 1839, just south of it.[34] Together they comprised an area of 264,938 statute acres bordered by county Galway to the west, county Offaly to the north and east and by Tipperary to the south (fig. 1).[35] These unions have been chosen as the focus of this study because they represent a large and a small union and while both were predominantly rural the area contains the town of Nenagh, one of the largest towns in north Tipperary, as well as several smaller towns. In 1881 these unions had a combined population of 40,562 which fell by 23.8 per cent to 30,891 by 1911, similar to the county average population decrease of 23.9 per cent.[36] Borrisokane union was made up of three dispensary districts: Borrisokane, Cloughjordan and Terryglass, with a dispensary station in each district and a workhouse with infirmary in Borrisokane.[37] Nenagh union had five dispensary districts: Nenagh, Newport, Portroe, Silvermines and Toomevara with seven dispensary stations, one in each district and two in Nenagh and Portroe.[38] This increased to eight in 1915 when Toomevara district got a second dispensary station in Templederry.[39] The workhouse, infirmary and fever hospital for the region were in Nenagh. Cloughjordan dispensary, the first to be established, was in existence from 1813; Nenagh dispensary was established in 1817 with a second dispensary built at Knigh, between Nenagh and the village of Puckane, in 1858; Borrisokane and Silvermines dispensaries opened in 1819; Newport and Toomevara in 1825 and Lorrha in 1829.[40] Lorrha district became Terryglass district in 1852; the dispensary for this district was moved from Lorrha to Carrigahorig between the aforementioned villages and on the border of these two parishes.[41] Portroe was a new dispensary area established after 1851 with dispensary stations in Portroe and Ballina.[42]

Toomevara was the first district in Nenagh union to have a midwife employed from 1894, while the first midwife in Borrisokane union was employed in Cloughjordan district from 1897.[43] When a dispensary midwife was not available to them, women called upon the assistance of the local 'handywoman' or unqualified midwife or her female relatives or neighbours, especially those who had given birth themselves, to aid her and see her safely through her confinement, which would take place in her own home.[44] The dispensary doctor had to be qualified in midwifery and could be called on to attend at a delivery, especially if it was difficult or there were complications following the birth.[45] By 1902, each of the dispensary districts in both unions employed a qualified midwife to assist women throughout pregnancy, delivery and in the antenatal period, in compliance with the instructions of the Local Government Board (LGB).[46] This topic will be explored further in Chapter 2.

The greatest changes wrought by the poor laws were in the establishment of a national network of buildings to accommodate the destitute poor, known as workhouses, which combined indoor relief for the destitute poor and medical relief in an infirmary or fever hospital for the sick destitute poor.[47] Nenagh workhouse, in the townland of Tyone, was opened in 1842 and had room for up to 1,000 inmates.[48] Borrisokane workhouse was opened in 1853 in the townland of Ballyhaden with room to accommodate up to 600 inmates.[49] Each poor-law union was managed by a board of guardians, made up of selected *ex-officio* members such as magistrates and justices of the peace, and elected members, who were ratepayers in the union.[50] Until 1896, when legislation was passed to allow for women to be guardians, all members of the board were men.[51] Nenagh would get its first 'lady guardians' in 1905 when Mabel Mary Frances Dease and Margaret Jane Powell were elected to the board.[52] The overall responsibility for the systems that existed under the poor laws sat with the LGB, which had taken over this power from the poor-law commissioners in 1872.[53] It set the rules, carried out inspections, audited the accounts and minute books of guardians' meetings and had the final say in all decisions made by the board, such as the hiring of staff and their salaries.[54] It was because of the rules enforced by the LGB that significant changes in nursing staff were seen from 1897.[55]

By 1881 the population of Ireland had plummeted from its high in 1841, the result of famine, disease and emigration.[56] In Tipperary, it had fallen by 54 per cent between these years, from 435,553 to 199,612. By 1911 the population had fallen another 23.6 per cent to 152,433, giving an overall decrease in population in the county between 1841 and 1911 of 65 per cent.[57] During this period there was also a reduction in pauperism and an increased willingness of the guardians of poor-law unions to assist people by the provision of outdoor relief. This meant that by 1881 there were very few people resident in the workhouses in Nenagh and Borrisokane in receipt of indoor relief when compared to the capacity of both houses and the numbers that had dwelt in them between 1846 and 1852.[58] By 1870 more than half of the admissions to Nenagh workhouses were sick people seeking treatment, while in Borrisokane the sick made up a quarter of the admissions.[59] Each workhouse had a medical officer attached to it, as well as men and women employed in the infirmaries and fever hospital to nurse the sick. Many of these 'nurses' were pauper inmates who received extra privileges, such as tobacco or extra rations, for the work they did. A limited number of paid nurses were employed, but few had any formal training or qualifications and there were often complaints regarding their behaviour and the care they provided.[60]

Improvements in the provision of care and the management of Nenagh workhouse infirmary came with the arrival of the Sisters of Mercy in 1882.[61] Nenagh board of guardians was keen to employ the nuns and did so as soon as a vacancy arose in the infirmary with two sisters taking up their posts in the female infirmary in July 1882.[62] The nuns received training to prepare them for their work in the workhouse but they were not trained nurses.[63] Nurse training for the nuns formed part of the reforms that began in 1897.[64] The Nenagh boards of guardians employed a qualified midwife to work as a night nurse in the male infirmary and to attend midwifery cases in 1897, after managing for several years without one, following increased pressure to do so from the LGB.[65] The board of guardians of Borrisokane union did not see the necessity of employing qualified nurses for the workhouse until 1901.[66] The work of nuns and nurses in the fever hospital and workhouse infirmary will be examined further in Chapter 3.

In 1900, tuberculosis, in all its forms, replaced 'old age' as the leading cause of death in Ireland, claiming 16,903 lives that year.[67] This was not a new disease, having existed for thousands of years, but it became the focus of public-health campaigns throughout the world in the late nineteenth and early twentieth centuries following the discovery of *Mycobacterium tuberculosis*, the bacterium that causes the disease, by Dr Robert Koch in 1882.[68] Prior to that, the disease was thought to be hereditary and therefore unpreventable.[69] The news that it was caused by a bacterium and was an infectious disease meant that it could be prevented and treated, though not everyone believed this new theory.[70] It became apparent that the only way to deal with the disease was by an approach that included prevention through a healthy diet, fresh air, good ventilation, cleanliness, banning spitting in public and separating the ill from the well.[71] From 1901 the LGB instructed boards of guardians that they must create separate wards in the infirmary for the care of patients with tuberculosis.[72] The first sanatorium in Ireland was built in Wicklow where the fresh mountain air was thought to be beneficial to patients, especially those with phthisis or pulmonary tuberculosis. Patients who were believed to have a chance of recovery could be sent there from all parts of Ireland, with the cost of their care covered by the union from which they came.[73] This 'white plague' was a cause that rallied many supporters and it provided a new platform for female philanthropy in the form of the Women's National Health Association (WNHA), established by Lady Ishbel Aberdeen in 1907. This association would have 180 branches throughout Ireland by 1909 with members active in raising awareness of tuberculosis, including how it could be prevented and how to stop it spreading. Through setting up District Nursing Associations (DNA) they fundraised to employ a district nurse in their area to provide home nursing to patients with tuberculosis.[74] The Nenagh branch of the WNHA established Nenagh Nursing Association and employed Mary Alice Doyle, a nurse trained under the Queen's Jubilee scheme, in 1909.[75] The work of the nurse and the issue of tuberculosis will be discussed in Chapter 4.

The history and evolution of nursing and midwifery have been written from many perspectives: as biography, as amateur historiography, in commemoration of an institution or organization and as memoir. In particular, Florence Nightingale left her own writings about nursing and has been the subject of numerous biographies and articles, most recently in celebration of her two-hundredth birthday in 2020.[76] Modern nurses and midwives have been involved in recording the history of their profession, such as those written in celebration of special anniversaries: 'Nursing and midwifery in Ireland in the twentieth century: fifty years of *An Bord Altranais* (the Nursing Board), 1950–2000' by Joseph Robins and 'A century of service: a history of the Irish Nurses and Midwives Organization, 1919–2019' by Mark Loughrey; or to commemorate the founding of an institution: 'St Vincent's Hospital, Dublin, 1834–1984' by H.J. Beckett. However, as Gerard Fealy highlights in his doctoral thesis, published as *A history of apprenticeship nurse training in Ireland* in 2006, 'there is a deficit of scholarly writing regarding the history of nursing in Ireland' and its associated social history.[77] Those historians who have published works on nursing and midwifery in an Irish context include Maria Luddy, Ciara Breathnach, Gerard Fealy and Margaret Preston, whose writings have influenced this work. Other eminent Irish historians writing about women's history, Irish nuns in the nineteenth century, medicine and charity, tuberculosis and the work of the Women's National Health Association – Maria Luddy, Caitriona Clear, Lawrence Geary, Frances Carruthers and others – have also influenced this work.

At a local level, the work of the Sisters of Mercy in Nenagh workhouse infirmary was celebrated in an article by local historian Nancy Murphy, which was printed in the *Nenagh Guardian* in 1982 to commemorate the centenary of the nuns' work in healthcare in the town.[78] This topic has also been written about in 'The Sisters of Mercy of Birr and Nenagh' by Sister Pius O'Brien, published in 1994. Of the other nurses and midwives featured in the following chapters, few have been written about before except in personal family histories. While their work was important, perhaps as it was largely viewed as 'women's work' and not highly esteemed, it has gone largely unrecorded. It is hoped that this study will contribute to the knowledge and understanding of the essential part that women played in health provision in the poor-law unions of Borrisokane and Nenagh between 1882 and 1922.

1. Professional nursing and midwifery in Nenagh and Borrisokane poor-law unions

Nursing and midwifery are two distinct and separate disciplines under the umbrella of 'nursing', a term used in its broadest context during the period being studied, 1882–1922, when it referred to most occupations that involved caring for children, the elderly or the sick. Many with the job title 'nurse' were domestic servants caring for the children of the household in which they were employed, while others were carers or companions to the elderly. A 'wet nurse' was a lactating woman who could be employed as a domestic servant in a house with a young baby or she might be employed by the poor-law union to foster children from the workhouse until they were older, or 'nurse' might describe someone employed in a hospital or who delivered babies.[1] Having the moniker 'nurse' did not mean that the owner held a professional qualification or had undergone any training for the role. The impetus to professionalize both hospital nursing and midwifery would see this change.

In the nineteenth century hospital nursing was a low-status job for the poorest people in society.[2] Some hospital nurses were former patients who stayed on and worked for their bed and board.[3] They had no training in caring for the sick, with their tasks equivalent to 'a specialized form of charring'.[4] Midwifery at this time was also a job mostly undertaken by poor women but it involved skills and knowledge that gave the local midwife, often referred to as a 'handywoman', 'helper-outer' or even 'rabbit-catcher', a level of respect and position within her community.[5] The majority of babies born in the nineteenth century were born at home with the midwife attending the birth there; even in cities such as Dublin, where maternity and lying-in hospitals were plentiful, home births were more common and safer than hospital delivery.[6] Being known to her neighbours as someone who had knowledge of medical matters, the handywoman might also be called on to conduct other tasks that involved intimate care of the body, such as laying out the dead, or caring for the sick.[7] Conversely, the versatility of the handywoman would be part of her undoing as she was accused of carrying disease from the sick and dead to the birthing room and being the cause of deaths from infection.[8] Campaigns to rid hospitals of untrained nurses and the community of its handywomen were part of the movements for nursing reform that started as early as the 1830s and would continue throughout the mid- to late nineteenth century.[9] Campaigners wanted to create an educated workforce of qualified nurses and midwives with an overarching goal of improved sanitation as well as providing better care for the sick and pregnant women, and a reduction in deaths from preventable causes such as infection.[10] There were many vested interests associated with this agenda, which Fealy tells us 'was part of a wider process of social change involving women and their role in society'.[11] Professionalization of hospital nursing was championed by three main groups: nurse reformers, hospital doctors and those seeking more and better employment opportunities for women, while those who sought training and registration for midwives included doctors in private practice and the government.[12]

Nurse reformers such as Florence Nightingale, regarded by many as the founder of modern nursing, promoted the development of nursing as an art and a science, where care, compassion and commitment were guided by scientific knowledge, such as the introduction of hygienic practices, especially hand washing, to prevent the spread of infection.[13] Hospital doctors wanted trained nurses to assist them who understood scientific practices and would follow their instructions with skill and without question, while those seeking to widen the very small pool of respectable occupations for women saw the reforms in nursing as the key to unlocking this field of work for middle- and upper-class women.[14] In reality it was the daughters of farmers and the skilled working classes who were attracted to the profession, with women of the upper classes acting in a supervisory capacity, often on a voluntary basis.[15] Luddy tells us that the issue of nursing reform was more prevalent in England than it was in Ireland, where nursing of the sick poor in the nineteenth century was predominantly undertaken by nuns, in particular by the Sisters of Charity, founded by Mary Aikenhead in 1815, and the Sisters of Mercy, founded by Catherine McCauley in 1831.[16] This was not applicable to midwifery as nuns were forbidden to practise midwifery by the rules of their orders until the middle of the twentieth century.[17]

Those clamouring for a professional body of midwives included doctors who complained of the dangers posed to pregnant women and their babies by traditional midwives or handywomen; more pertinently perhaps, they saw these untrained independent practitioners as their competition for patients, who often chose the more affordable handywoman over the medical man.[18] In the places of male power – parliament, the medical profession and the Local Government Board – handywomen midwives were spoken of in derogatory terms and blamed for causing injury and costing the lives of mothers and babies, but in the homes of the poor the handywoman was often the preferred birth attendant.[19] A fictional character, Mrs Sarah Gamp, created by Charles Dickens in *Martin Chuzzlewit*, published in 1843, came to represent all that was wrong with traditional midwives and domiciliary nurses. She was a drunkard, stole from her employers, was loud, brash and foul mouthed and was neglectful of her patients.[20] It was an image so strong and well publicized that it endures to the modern day in nursing histories and textbooks as the antithesis of what a good nurse should be.[21] However, as Anne Summer says in defence of those women who Sarah Gamp was meant to represent,

> since few of Sarah's fellow-workers wrote their own letters, much less their autobiographies, the task of rescuing them from 'the enormous condescension of posterity' is not an easy one. But the thousands of women whose honest livelihood consisted in caring, kindly and decently, for their fellow creatures, deserve more respectful attention from historians of medicine and of women's work than they have hitherto received.[22]

The Victorians believed that women had a natural instinct for nursing and the innate ability to be nurses but conversely determined that, to be effective, nurses had to undergo increasingly specialized and technical training before they were deemed acceptable workers for the health system.[23] The reformers took great pains to convince the public that nurses needed to be properly trained and state registered to protect the helpless sick from malpractice.[24] An integral part of those campaigns was to discredit one type of nurse while extolling the many virtues of the other. This led to handywomen midwives and untrained nurses being portrayed as ugly, drunken, slovenly, low-class women who spread puerperal fever, caused unnecessary torture and fatal consequences for their patients, while their trained counterparts were depicted as 'strong, moral, kind, gentle, personable, diligent, intelligent, womanly, and, above all, obedient'.[25]

The campaign to regulate the training and practice of midwives in Britain eventually resulted in the passing of the Midwives Act, 1902, which established the Central Midwives Board with jurisdiction over midwives in England and Wales. This was followed by the Midwives (Scotland) Act, 1915, and the Midwives (Ireland) Act, 1918, which established similar boards in Scotland and in Ireland.[26] The act prohibited unqualified and unregistered women from practising midwifery. The Nurses Registration (Ireland) Act, 1919, was passed at the same time as similar acts for England, Wales and Scotland.

All of these arguments and campaigns, combined with the workhouse-reform agenda, would appear to have had some effect in the poor-law unions of Borrisokane and Nenagh. The overall numbers of nurses and midwives were small but there was a significant increase between 1901 and 1911, especially of those employed in poor-law medical services. The 1891 census recorded only fifty women in county Tipperary 'connected with the medical profession': thirty-five midwives and fifteen women working in 'subordinate medical service'.[27] There were also fifty-four women working in a 'hospital or institution service'. That is a total of 104 out of a population of 173,188. By the 1901 census there was an overall decrease in nurses and midwives but as the population had also decreased, to 160,232, this amounted to no change in the percentage of women engaged in health provision.[28] According to the 1901 census, 411 people in Tipperary returned their occupation as 'nurse'. Their ages ranged from 12 to 90 years. By 1911 the number of people in the county had dropped to 152,433, with 478 returning their occupation as 'nurse'. However, not all who called themselves nurses were involved in health provision. A closer examination of the data reveals the majority of those who identified as nurses were involved in domestic service, predominantly caring for children, with some involved in caring for the elderly. In

"FIFTY   YEARS."

2. The difference fifty years makes: the nurse in 1838 and in 1888
(from *Nursing Record*, vol. 1 (20 Dec. 1888), p. 537)

1901 this amounted to 260 women or 63.3 per cent of the nurses.
The ninety-six nurses who worked in health provision accounted for
only 23.3 per cent of the total, with a further fifty-five women or
13.4 per cent for whom the type of nursing they were doing could
not be determined from the census information. By 1911 there was an
overall increase in the number of women returning their occupation
as 'nurse', with the percentage who were involved in health provision
more than doubling in ten years to 215 women or 45 per cent.[29] This
significant increase still represents low numbers of nurses.

The nurses who cared for the sick and infirm or were involved
in midwifery identified themselves in several ways: 'fever nurse',
'night nurse', 'hospital nurse', 'hospital trained nurse', 'professional
nurse', 'nurse fever hospital', 'nurse in workhouse', 'night nurse
in workhouse', 'trained nurse', 'qualified nurse', 'infirmary nurse',
'nurse', 'mental nurse', 'male nurse', 'nurse of medical hall', 'Queen's
nurse', 'district nurse', 'midwife and lady's nurse', 'maternity nurse'
'infant nurse and midwife', 'midwife' and 'private midwife'.[30] This
equates to four main categories of nurses: general nurse, mental nurse,
midwife and district nurse. All but three of those who identified their
occupation as nurse were female.

A further break-down of these numbers to those living and working in the poor-law unions of Nenagh and Borrisokane identifies only twenty-four nurses returned for 1901 and thirty-eight in 1911, even after variances in how people returned themselves are taken into account; for example, the nuns working in Nenagh workhouse infirmary in 1901 were returned as 'Sister of Mercy' and not as nurses.[31] The majority were employed either as dispensary midwives or in the workhouse infirmaries of each union (Appendix 1). It would appear at first glance that there were very few midwives, as only four women returned their occupation as 'midwife' in 1901 and six in 1911, but on closer examination it is evident that many midwives called themselves 'nurse', including most of the dispensary midwives and those in private practice such as Margaret Daughton, who returned her occupation in 1911 as 'professional nurse' though the birth registers for Nenagh in 1906 and 1919 show she was practising midwifery.[32]

Analysis of the data from the summary of the 1891 census and the more detailed records of the 1901 and 1911 census identifies some interesting findings. One similarity across all years is that while the nurses were predominantly Roman Catholic, the proportion of Protestants who became nurses was higher than their numbers in the general population in Tipperary. Based on the census records of 1911, the ratio of Catholics to all Protestant religions in the general population was 18 to 1 whereas the ratio among nurses was as low as 7.5 to 1 in 1901 and as high as 12 to 1 in 1891. A significant difference from 1891 to the subsequent years was the literacy rates, with moderate levels of illiteracy in 1891 and almost total literacy in subsequent years. This could be reflective of more girls getting the opportunity of primary education but it also indicates that there were a significant number of untrained nurses and midwives working in 1891, as to complete training and examinations the nurses would need to be literate. The age profile was much lower in 1901 and 1911 compared to 1891, when there were equal numbers of nurses aged 25 to 45 and 45 to 65, with a significant number aged over 65 years, whereas in 1901 and 1911 the majority of the nurses were aged 25 to 45 with fewer in any of the other age categories. The number of unmarried women, including the Sisters of Mercy, was double the combined numbers of married and widowed women, which shows that, while marriage was not a barrier to being a nurse or midwife, it was a profession dominated by single women. It may also be reflective of the young age-profile of the nurses, some of whom were married after the 1911 census.[33] The statistic that is perhaps most surprising is that approximately a third of the women were not native to Tipperary but had been born in other counties or countries. This suggests that women were prepared to move to where the jobs were, which will be examined further in Chapters 2 and 3.

The socio-economic background of the nurses was not evident from the census records in all cases, but it was possible by cross-referencing with marriage and birth records to determine this for thirty-two of the nurses and future nurses listed in appendices 1, 2. The socio-economic class of the nurses is based on their fathers' occupation. The majority of the nurses were from farming backgrounds, which accounted for nineteen nurses or 59 per cent of the total. The next highest representation was among the daughters of labourers and skilled workers, who accounted for 19 per cent or six nurses. The rest were daughters of a sea captain, a policeman, a soldier, a shopkeeper and an engine driver. These findings are in line with what Margaret Preston and other authors have said about nurses' social backgrounds.[34] An exception was Janet Bruce, whose father was an army major and later magistrate, justice of the peace and member of Borrisokane board of guardians.[35]

2. Handywomen, midwives and the dispensary system

Childbirth is a natural part of the cycle of life during which women have supported each other through the millennia. The usual birth attendants included mother, sisters, aunts, friends, neighbours and the local midwife, a woman who was known to be skilled in assisting a mother through pregnancy, delivery and afterwards. For most of history, midwives have been women who held no specific education or qualifications but who understood the processes of childbirth from practice and experience.[1] In Ireland, as elsewhere, these midwives were often referred to as 'handywomen'. Regrettably, their lives have not been studied because, as historians of women's history such as Breathnach tell us, it is difficult to find documentary evidence of them as they did not leave written accounts of their lives and their work. The handywoman would retain her popularity as birth attendant until late in the nineteenth century and into the twentieth century, though the numbers of qualified midwives were increasing throughout the latter half of the nineteenth century and pressure was coming to regulate the practice of all midwives.[2] Legislation governing the practices of midwives was slow in coming to Ireland, where the Midwives (Ireland) Act was not passed until 1918, sixteen years after similar legislation had been introduced in England and Wales and more than a hundred years after Austria, Norway, Sweden (1801), France (1803) and Belgium (1818).[3] Pressure to pass the act came from those who blamed the high levels of maternal deaths from infection and haemorrhage on the unhygienic practices of untrained midwives and wanted to see an end to their 'execrable traffic in the lives of parturient women'.[4] The death rate of women due to pregnancy-related haemorrhage or infection in Ireland in 1882 was 1 per 128 births.[5]

Prior to 1882 the women of Nenagh poor-law union had access to midwives, including some who had qualifications. Even the poorest women of Nenagh had the services of a dispensary midwife to call on. In 1840, prior to the reorganization of the dispensary system under the 1851 act, Nenagh dispensary employed Ellen Hayes as midwife to attend the poor women of the district at a salary of £8 per annum, for which she conducted seventy-three deliveries in that year.[6] In her own words though, she was not a midwife but a 'knowledgeable woman'.[7] She was replaced in 1842 by Mary Akins, who conducted forty-one deliveries that year and forty-five deliveries in 1844.[8] A midwife continued to be employed in Nenagh dispensary up to 1851, though the post was lost with the reorganization of the dispensary districts.[9] Akins had not left town though, as she was advertising her services as 'accoucheur and ladies nurse-tender' in 1859 and she was still attending births in 1870.[10] In 1865, Catherine McLoughlin, resident in Graces Street, Nenagh, advertised that she held a diploma from the Dublin Lying-In Hospital and was available as a 'ladies nurse-tender' with references from local doctors.[11] The birth registers for 1875 and 1882 show that she was working as a midwife in Nenagh then.[12] In 1871, Mrs Quigly, 36 Barrack Street, Nenagh, advertised her availability as 'midwife and nurse' to the 'ladies of Limerick, Clare and Tipperary'. She had 'been connected with' Limerick Lying-in Hospital and was setting up in private practice as a midwife and monthly nurse.[13]

Apart from those who advertised or whose names appeared in the newspaper, sometimes as witnesses in maternal death or infanticide cases, it is possible to identify other midwives and handywomen from birth registers.[14] Under the Registration of Births and Deaths (Ireland) Act, 1863, Part III, Section 31 all births of children born in Ireland after 31 December 1863 had to be registered within twenty-one days of the birth by either the parents, the occupier of the house in which the child was born, the nurse or any person present at the birth.[15] In most cases the father or the mother registered the birth but in other cases the nurse or person who attended the birth did so. In many instances the registrar made this clear by recording their name and 'nurse present at birth'. From this set of data a number of names present themselves as candidates for the midwives and handywomen in the poor-law unions of Nenagh and Borrisokane. The table in Appendix 3 identifies many of them from specifically chosen years between 1870 and 1919. 1870, 1875 and 1882 show what was occurring in the unions in the years before and up to the start date of this study; 1896 and 1906 were chosen as they are at the five-year interval between the census, and 1919 is the last year for which birth records are publicly available at present. It does not by any means capture all of the midwives working in the area nor does it identify whether they were qualified. They have been included if their name was recorded on the birth register as 'present at birth' more than once or where the registrar has written 'nurse' in the register. The registers show certain names that featured frequently in the years 1870–82; in particular, Mary Green, Catherine Moore and Margaret O'Brien from Nenagh and Anne Keef/O'Keeffe from Newport. Each of these women was recorded as attending at least twenty deliveries in the years assessed in which they were still practising. Anne Keef, who died in 1885 aged 85 years, was still working in 1882.[16] There were fewer nurses notifying births in Borrisokane union, with the exception of Biddy Ryan from Borrisokane, who is recorded as the nurse in attendance at births in 1870, 1875 and 1882.

Dispensary doctors, known as 'medical officers', were requesting the services of 'properly qualified midwives' in dispensary districts from the 1860s because of the problems they encountered when untrained handywomen attended their patients.[17] In 1869 the registrar in Shinrone, Kings County, near Cloughjordan district, asserted that a quarter of the cases he was called to were 'due to the dangerous mode adopted by inexperienced hands'.[18] In 1877 Nenagh board of guardians discussed the possibility of employing a midwife for the union but Dr Patrick Harty Cleary, of Queen's Street, Nenagh, felt there should be one in every district.[19] Silvermines district advertised for a midwife several times throughout 1877 but there were very few applicants and none was suitable.[20] The LGB annual report for 1882 says that a midwife was sanctioned for the Silvermines district but had not been appointed.[21]

By 1882 there were three dispensary medical officers in Borrisokane union and six in Nenagh union.[22] Each medical officer was responsible for attending the dispensary at set times to treat patients with dispensary tickets, also referred to as 'black tickets' because they were written in black ink, which allowed them free medical advice and medicines at the dispensary.[23] The medical officers also attended more serious cases in the patient's home on a visiting or 'red' ticket. This included attending deliveries when they were called to do so. The medical officer could not refuse to attend a patient on a red ticket.[24]

The services available to pregnant women in the poor-law unions of Borrisokane and Nenagh in 1882 included attending the dispensary doctor, if they were eligible, and engaging the local handywoman midwife or they could choose to deliver their baby with the help of a female relative or neighbour or without any assistance at all. Hospital delivery was possible but not common and often more dangerous than delivery at home, the place that reformers such as Nightingale declared to be the safest and best place for birth to take place.[25] It was also possible to attend the workhouse infirmary for delivery but the low numbers of births occurring in either of the infirmaries in Nenagh or Borrisokane indicate that this was not a popular choice, with an average of eight births a year occurring in Nenagh and one a year in Borrisokane between 1893 and 1914.[26]

The poor-law commissioners had supported the employment of midwives in large dispensary districts where the number of deliveries every year justified it and when the LGB took over from them they continued with the mission of increasing their numbers.[27] The annual report of the LGB for 1903 shows the progress of their efforts to ensure that 'the poor in every dispensary district in Ireland will be enabled eventually to obtain the services of competent midwives'.[28]

Table 1. Number of midwives employed in dispensary districts in Ireland, 1853–1903

Year	No. of midwives
1853	10
1863	63
1873	196
1883	287
1893	361
1903	551

(source: Thirty-first annual report of the LGB, 1903)[29]

As the nineteenth century ended and the twentieth began, the dispensary medical officers in Nenagh and Borrisokane unions got what they had requested with the appointment of qualified midwives to each district. The first evidence for a qualified midwife employed in the dispensary system of Nenagh union relates to *c.*1894 when Anne

McDonald, a widow and native of Clonmel, moved to Toomevara with her children to take up the post of dispensary midwife.[30] She would carry out her duties in the district for twenty years until her retirement in 1914, at which time her daughter Mary replaced her.[31] On her retirement she was commended for her hard work and that in all that time she had 'never got a day's leave'.[32] This tells something of the conditions under which the district midwives worked. They were not entitled to paid leave but were required to pay for their replacement if they took leave as the district could not be left unattended.[33] This situation would not change until after 1919 when the Irish Nurses Union was formed and fought for better wages and conditions for nurses, including paid annual leave.[34] It was only when they were on certified sick leave that the board of guardians might cover the cost of their replacement.[35] Borrisokane union employed an unqualified midwife for Cloughjordan district from 1897 who was replaced by Kathleen Diver from Donegal in 1898, the first qualified midwife in that union.[36] Diver resigned in 1902 with the intention of moving to South Africa.[37]

These midwives would have created competition for the handywomen who were already providing a service in the districts. The 1896 birth registers show a number of them working in Nenagh: Bridget Boney, Catherine Moore and Winifred Hogan being the most active, but none of them was as busy as Mary Mangan in Newport who attended over thirty deliveries that year. She was not found on the 1901 census and therefore not counted among the midwives in Nenagh union in Appendix 1. She died in 1902 aged 55 years, her occupation recorded as 'midwife'.[38] This is worth noting, as the official records do not use the term 'handywoman'; they say 'nurse' or 'midwife'. The exception is found in the death records of some of those who in life had been recorded as 'nurse' but on the death register their occupation was given as 'domestic servant', such as Judy Hough from Borrisokane, or 'labourer's widow' as in the case of Anne Keef.[39]

The dispensary midwives were paid an annual wage, which in 1902 was between £20 and £25 per annum, sometimes with accommodation included.[40] If they lived in the dispensary they got an allowance of coal for use on dispensary clinic days but not for their own use and if they took on the role of dispensary caretaker they received additional payment.[41] Their salary was twice that of an unqualified midwife but it was still considered a low wage.[42] This was partly because their work as dispensary midwives was meant to be a part-time job, even though they could be called on at any time, day or night. It was expected that they would also take on private cases in the district for which they would be paid by the patient.[43] The success of their private practice varied greatly across the unions. Rosaline Waterson, from Meath and Kildare, was the Nenagh midwife from 1902 to 1919.[44] She was appointed ahead of others because as well as the required qualifications she had three years' experience from the Coombe Maternity and Lying-in Hospital, Dublin.[45] This was the busiest district in Nenagh union, with two dispensary stations and about three times as many deliveries each year as the other districts, yet when she took up her post she was on the lowest salary in the union at £20 per annum. The extent of her district work and the competition posed by the number of independent midwives in the town of Nenagh prevented her from developing a profitable private practice. Another obstacle for her was that many of the places that the dispensary midwife had to visit on tickets were in a 'poor state' and private patients were not inclined to employ a nurse who 'has to go to such places'.[46] Likewise, Kathleen Heffernan, a widow and mother of five, was appointed to Terryglass district in October 1910 but resigned within the year because the annual salary of £25 was insufficient for her to support herself and her family.[47] By contrast, Helen Kelly, the district midwife for Borrisokane and Terryglass from *c.*1900 and Borrisokane only from 1910 to 1947, had such a large and profitable private practice that by 1945 she had opened a maternity nursing home in her house, registered as Mrs Kelly's Nursing Home at *Bella Vista*, Borrisokane.[48] There were only two such services in north Tipperary, the other was Nurse Tompkins' Nursing Home opened in Kenyon Street, Nenagh in 1930.[49] Helen Kelly also had the advantage of being a 'local', having been born in Rathcabbin, and there do not appear to have been as many independent midwives working in her district.[50] She was the longest-serving midwife in the Borrisokane union when she retired after forty-seven years.[51] Mary McSoley, the midwife in the Silvermines district, had the same length of service when she retired in 1947, making her the longest-serving midwife in Nenagh union.[52]

A condition of their employment was that they had to live in the
district to be close at hand when called on to attend a birth. In 1905,
when Mary Anne Nolan was appointed to Portroe district she was
required to live in the town of Portroe as 'there were a great many
poor people living there and around the Quarries'. However, when
she moved there she was met with animosity as 'there were so many
private practitioners that she was not wanted' so she returned to live
in Ballina, at the outer limits of the district.[53] Where she lived became
an ongoing issue for the board of guardians who insisted she live in
Portroe or resign her post.[54] A compromise was eventually reached
in 1910 when it was agreed that she could continue to live in Ballina
and cover the lower portion of the district while a second midwife
would be employed for Portroe town and environs.[55] This clause also
caused a problem for Helen Kelly, who had covered two districts for
ten years, but was required to resign from Terryglass district in 1911
as she lived in Borrisokane.[56]

By 1909 there were qualified midwives attached to each
dispensary district in both unions. The birth registers for 1906 and
1919 show a greater prominence in deliveries performed by the
dispensary midwives: Rosaline Waterson (Nenagh), Bridget Hogan
(Cloughjordan), Kate Kyte (Newport), Helen Kelly (Borrisokane/
Terryglass), Katherine Wheally (Newport), Mary McSoley (Silvermines),
Josephine. B. Carey (Portroe), Anne McDonald (Toomevara), Annie
Lyons (Nenagh) and Mary O'Donoghue (Toomevara). Some of the
handywomen were still active in these years, in particular Bridget
Boney Walsh who was attending births up to 1919. In 1918 it became
illegal for any midwife who was not registered under the Registration
of Midwives (Ireland) Act, 1918, to attend a woman in labour and
delivery but this new law was not yet being enforced in 1919. Bridget
Boney Walsh had more than twenty years of experience by that
time. She had been employed periodically in the workhouse and in
the district before 1900 but when she replaced Rosaline Waterson,
who was on sick leave in 1907, the LGB queried why an 'unqualified
midwife' had been called on to attend a case.[57] She might not have
been an acceptable employee in the eyes of the LGB but she appears
to have been held in high esteem in Nenagh where she was known to
be hard working, industrious, competent and well liked.[58] The birth
records also show the emergence of qualified midwives in private

practice such as Margaret Daughton, Elizabeth de Clare, Mary Ellen McCormack, Sarah Teehan and Bridget Tomkins. These midwives were employed temporarily by the union to replace the dispensary midwives when they were on leave and could only do so if they had the required qualifications.[59]

Each midwife's caseload varied greatly but Nenagh district was by far the busiest in that union. Rosaline Waterson attended eighty-seven 'ticket cases' in 1915; fifty-seven cases in 1916, and twenty-six cases in the first three months of 1917.[60] In 1920 Annie Lyons, who had replaced Rosaline Waterson in 1919, attended fifty-two cases in a year; Kate Kyte, seventeen; Josephine Carey, ten; Mary Anne Nolan, seven; Mary McSoley, ten; and Mary Donohue, seventeen.[61] Each case involved between three and five visits before, during and after birth.[62]

The rationale for employing qualified midwives in the dispensary districts was to improve the standards of midwifery care for the poorest women and to reduce the number of maternal deaths. By 1908 positive reports were being made of their good work to this end. Mabel Dease said of Rosaline Waterson that

> since she had come to the district she had changed the old order of things for the better. The fever generally following the cases, it was her duty to attend, was now almost entirely unknown, as she insisted on cleanliness. She also insisted on the abolition of the habit of giving drink to patients, and this practice was quite discontinued in the locality under her charge.[63]

The quantifiable evidence of the effectiveness of qualified midwives was to be found in the reduction in maternal deaths. In 1901, one woman per 161 births died of pregnancy and birth-related problems; five year later, in 1906, that number had marginally reduced to one in 167 births. By this time there was a significant number of qualified midwives working in both unions, in either the dispensary system or in private practice. A very marked reduction in maternal death was seen in 1911 when it was one in 198 births and though it increased to one in 181 in 1916 it was down again to one in 199 in 1921.[64] The midwives were not the only contributing factor in this reduction in deaths, but their hygienic practices substantially reduced infection rates. Maternal deaths from haemorrhage and other 'accidents of birth', however, remained high.

The continuing desire to make labour and delivery safer for mothers and their babies would see a move to nursing-home or hospital births from this period, so that by 1946 the two nursing homes mentioned above as well as Nenagh hospital, formerly the workhouse infirmary, were registered and operating as maternity homes.[65]

3. Nuns, nurses and the workhouse

The workhouse system of indoor relief for the destitute poor, established under the Poor Relief (Ireland) Act, 1838, mirrored a similar system already operating in England and Wales under the Poor Law Amendment Act, 1834. The system was hated from its inception until the poor-law unions and workhouses were abolished under the Local Government (Temporary Provisions) Act, 1923. It was, however, acknowledged that the system was better than nothing when 'some measure of relief was necessary for the teeming misery of Ireland in the early part of the nineteenth century'.[1] The Medical Charities Act, 1851, brought medical relief for the destitute poor under the poor laws, which included treatment in workhouse infirmaries and fever hospitals. These services were extended to all sick poor and not just the destitute poor under the Poor Relief (Ireland) Act, 1862, so that by the end of the nineteenth century a comprehensive, albeit imperfect, public-health system existed in Ireland.

Geary asserts that there was as much aversion to using the poor-law hospitals as there was in being admitted to the workhouse, leading those who could afford to do so to access the county infirmary or voluntary hospitals in the cities.[2] This aversion probably existed for people in the poor-law unions of Borrisokane and Nenagh too but it did not prevent them from accessing the poor-law medical services, as can be seen from the records of the numbers treated.[3] The combination of poor road networks and long distances made the county infirmary in Cashel or the hospitals in the nearest city, Limerick, impractical options especially in an emergency. The convenience of utilizing the services that were in their vicinity made the poor-law institutions both a logical and a prudent choice, particularly for those who were entitled to free treatment. There were other medical services available in both unions for those who could afford to pay for them including private medical practitioners, such as those who advertised in trade directories or the midwives and handywomen discussed in Chapter 2.

Folk cures, charms and herbal remedies were also popular throughout the country along with attending healers and bonesetters, according to the stories recounted in the school's collection of the Irish folklore commission.[4]

As the nineteenth century progressed the level of pauperism fell throughout Ireland, resulting in a reduction of inmates in workhouses, while simultaneously the workhouse infirmaries became an important part of the public-health system. Dispensary doctors were more inclined to refer ill patients to the infirmary for treatment than they had been.[5] With this increased focus on treating the sick as opposed to just maintaining the poor, came the need to improve the type and number of nurses working in the system. One of the rules of the workhouse was that anyone who was able to work must do so as a contribution to their maintenance within the workhouse. It then fell to male and female inmates who were fit enough for the work to undertake nursing duties in the infirmary, whether they were suited to this work or not. These untrained 'pauper nurses' worked under the supervision of the matron, who was likewise untrained in the care of the sick.[6] They were seen as one of the great evils of the system, described as selfish and ignorant, 'restrained by no sense of decency or religion, loud-voiced, quarrelsome and abusive'.[7] They were accused of neglect and abuse of patients, charging them for basic care such as the provision of meals and failing to provide any care if payment in money or kind was not forthcoming.[8]

It was into this system that the Sisters of Mercy brought their influence of order, cleanliness and economy in 1861, starting in Limerick. It would be another twenty years before Nenagh workhouse benefitted from their presence as employees of the workhouse, though they began visiting the paupers 'of their own creed' from 1864.[9] By 1880 the board of guardians of Nenagh workhouse were faced with a nursing problem. There were only two paid nurses: the recently married Bridget Reynolds, the fever hospital nurse, who had taken over the role from her aged mother, Bridget Carroll, on her death in July 1880, and Mrs Molloy, a widow and qualified midwife employed as infirmary nurse since 1877.[10] There had been some complaints about Molloy, each of which she refuted. In 1880 she had been brought before the board after being accused of drunkenness and neglect of a child in the infirmary and on another occasion in 1881 she was accused by a patient's daughter of neglecting her 70-year-old mother.[11] The daughter claimed that she found her mother, who was blind, bedridden and a patient of the infirmary for the past two years, cold and dirty, her person and bed clothes infested with vermin. She had one sheet beneath her but none covering her and the bed linen had not been changed for three weeks. When questioned about this, Molloy replied that it was not unusual for the linen to be changed once every three weeks.[12]

By 1881 the board of guardians was keen to employ the Sisters of Mercy as soon as a vacancy arose in the infirmary. Such an opportunity would present in March 1881. Molloy was asked to resign her post as infirmary nurse after being brought before the board for being under the influence of liquor while on duty. She admitted that she had consumed porter but denied that she was drunk. Following Molloy's resignation it was agreed that she would be replaced by two nurses. James O'Meara was particularly keen to open up the positions to the Sisters of Mercy, referring to their work in Limerick, Kilrush, Thurles and other unions where 'the good nuns acted in the humble capacity of nurses, and were looked on by the inmates of those houses as "ministering angels"'.[13] To that end, an advertisement appeared in the *Nenagh Guardian* on 16 April 1881.

Only one tender was received and that was from the Sisters of Mercy in Nenagh who proposed to take up the two nurse positions in the female infirmary. The rule of their order was that four nuns would come to form a community, when suitable apartments had been prepared for them, though only two sisters would be paid.[14] This made the nuns a cost-effective resource to the workhouse, which added to their desirability with the board who were intent on carrying out their duties without increasing the rates.[15] While they waited for the accommodation to be built by Mr Hanley, the nuns went to Tipperary workhouse to be trained by the sisters there.[16] The accommodation was ready in April 1882 and a small community was established by the two sisters who had been appointed to the posts: Jane Needham and Sophia Kennedy, both of whom were professed in 1873 as Sister Mary Gabriel and Sister Agnes respectively, Sister Mary Benedicta Quinn, possibly the mother superior of the community, and Sister Stanislaus Connors.[17] They acted as the nurses in the female infirmary and as supervisors in the male infirmary until July

1882, when the nurse there resigned.[18] In August, Teresa Daly (Sister Margaret) took up duty as head nurse in the male infirmary with Mary Finn employed as assistant to her in the male infirmary and midwife for the female infirmary.[19] Within a short time improvements were effected in patient care, diet, general order and cleanliness.[20] The board must have thought that all of their problems with nurses were over, but that was not the case. The nuns made a significant difference to the lives of the patients but they did not do night duty, finishing work each night at 9 o'clock. They were forbidden by their vows from carrying out certain duties such as midwifery, some surgeries and intimate care of male patients and, crucially, they were not trained nurses.[21] Day nursing was not the issue as when the nuns were on duty they were seen to be a good influence on both paid and pauper nurses, which ensured proper patient care.[22] Difficulties arose as a result of inadequate nursing care at night, when the wards were in the hands of pauper attendants alone. The medical officer in Nenagh workhouse, Dr Joshua Robert Minnitt, who held the post from 1874 to 1919, was in favour of trained nurses being employed in the infirmary and raised this with the board many times.[23] In 1888 he said that even though there were now fewer patients in the infirmary than several years previous, the patients they now had needed more nurses caring for them and he called for an inquiry to determine how many nurses were needed. Board members, at that time, implied that many of the patients were only in the infirmary because of the brandy they received as treatment for bronchitis and did not require more trained nurses to care for them.[24] In 1890 Minnitt complained that 'there is no trained nurse in the house at all'.[25]

Dr Browne, the LGB inspector for Nenagh, was concerned with what he found regarding nursing staff in the infirmary during his inspection in 1895 as outlined in his report:

> In the female infirmary, where there are at present forty patients distributed through twelve wards, there are two nuns and pauper attendants for day duty as nurses. The attendants sleep in the wards and look after the patients at night. There is also a pauper nurse, whose duty it is to visit the several wards during the night, and look after the patients. In the male infirmary there are three wards, with thirty-three patients, one nun, one

paid assistant and three pauper nurses to look after the patients' wants during the day. The three pauper assistants sleep in the wards, and attend the patients during the night. There is also a pauper assistant, whose duty it is to visit the wards during the night, and attend to any patients requiring his services. In the fever hospital there is one paid nurse. There have been no patients for a considerable time, and when necessary, nurse assistance is obtained. I consider it necessary that a paid night nurse should be appointed to the female infirmary, also one for the male infirmary.

The board of guardians were not in agreement with this and instead appointed two night nurses from among the pauper inmates, 'after careful selection', on a one-month trial. If that was not successful they would consider carrying out the suggestions of the LGB. During the review, Minnitt and some members of the board expressed their preference of employing trained nurses for night duty. Minnitt stated that there were 'a number of cases where old infirm patients in the infirmary had fallen out of their beds in the night', that night nursing was inadequate and a paid night nurse was required.[26] The board discussed the possibility of engaging a trained nurse for night duty but abandoned the idea because they felt that the inmates who had been appointed were doing their duties and were found to be satisfactory.[27]

At the same time as the night nursing issue was being discussed, the board had other nursing problems with the fever hospital. The appointed nurse, Bridget Reynolds, had lived with her husband Michael, the workhouse schoolmaster, and their children Bridget Mary and John Thomas in staff accommodation in the workhouse compound until 1893. When Michael retired in that year, however, following more than twenty years' service, he and the children were required to quit the workhouse and find lodgings in the town.[28] They were permitted to visit Bridget, who lived in the fever hospital, but could not stay there. When Michael became ill in 1895 he returned to live with Bridget in her quarters so that she could take care of him but this was done without the knowledge of the master or the permission of the guardians. Michael's presence there became known only when Minnitt was called to examine him. Bridget was brought before the board to account for her actions. They were not sympathetic to her explanation and called for her resignation in early June 1895.[29] Michael died in the workhouse on 23 June 1895 aged 58 years old from chronic bronchitis and cardiac syncope.[30] In an act of compassion, board member Thomas O'Brien proposed that Bridget be forgiven and her resignation be rescinded, which motion was carried.[31] She had plans to leave soon to go to her sister in Australia but being able to retain her post in the meantime would ensure that she and her children had a means of support until then. Following further inquiries in August 1895, however, she was again asked to leave her post.[32]

The board were pleased to appoint Alice Cahalan, a qualified nurse and daughter of Dr Michael Cahalan, as fever hospital nurse in September 1895.[33] Sadly, Alice would hold the post for less than a year before her untimely death from meningitis on 28 August 1896 aged 26 years. She died as a patient in Nenagh fever hospital.[34] Her death was followed a few weeks later by that of the assistant nurse of the fever hospital, Margaret Flannery, who died in the workhouse infirmary from cancer of the breast, aged 40, on 30 September 1896.[35] These deaths give credence to an unaccredited statement that was printed in the *Nenagh News* in 1896, warning of the risk posed to nurses, saying that 'a healthy girl of seventeen, devoting herself to hospital nursing, dies on average twenty-one years sooner than a girl of the same age moving among the general population'.[36] Miss Lavery, from Kilkenny, was then appointed to the post but resigned in August 1897 to take up a similar post in Roscrea union at an increased salary.[37] For the next few years the posts of nurse and assistant nurse of the fever hospital were rolled over frequently. Nurse Lavery was replaced by Maria Hickey, who was in turn replaced by Letitia Fennelly, who left in 1899 for a job in Bandon union at a higher salary.[38] When the post was advertised in 1900 at a salary of £25 per year with rations and apartments, it was also stated that 'the number of fever patients treated in the last year did not exceed twenty-five'.[39] Even with these low numbers, nursing in the fever hospital was arduous and potentially dangerous as exposure to infectious diseases left these nurses at risk of illness. At times when the fever hospital was free of patients the nurses worked in the main infirmary but when they had patients they were confined to the fever hospital and were not allowed near the main workhouse, infirmary, kitchen or any other buildings in case they spread disease.[40] There were even complaints about them attending mass in town where they might spread disease to the congregation.[41]

Another challenge that arose in the fever hospital was that when there was an outbreak of disease such as measles, scarlatina, typhus or similar then the two nurses appointed to the fever hospital were insufficient to do all the nursing that was required. For example, in 1894, an outbreak of typhoid fever in the town affected at least four Royal Irish Constabulary (RIC) officers, leading to the death of Constable Follis. The district inspector, Mr Rogers, wanted another nurse available to care for the three policemen who remained in the hospital. The board had received a letter from Bridget Reynolds requesting an extra nurse to assist her as she was exhausted, but the chairman responded by saying that 'Mrs Reynolds is a paid nurse, and she ought to do relay duty with her assistant; she ought to do either day or night duty'.[42] This meant that each lady was expected to work a twelve-hour shift, day or night, seven days a week with perhaps only the assistance of a reluctant pauper nurse. The paupers sometimes refused to do the work, especially in the fever hospital, for fear of getting sick themselves. In 1882 three female paupers in Nenagh workhouse were charged at the petty sessions for their refusal to assist the fever nurse.[43]

Pauper nurses were viewed as 'the blackest spot on the poor-law administration' and the sick poor deserved better.[44] By 1896, the Irish Medical Association, church hierarchy and Irish Workhouse Association were calling for reforms that included the cessation of pauper nursing, employment of trained nurses, nurse training for nuns, better diets for all inmates, better care of the children in the nurseries, more humane conditions for elderly and infirm inmates and improved sanitary facilities.[45] These reforms were supported by the LGB who instructed the boards of guardians that pauper nurses were prohibited in workhouse infirmaries under the Nursing Order of 1897 and that trained nurses were required in the infirmary under a further Nursing Order in 1898.[46] The Nenagh board of guardians was reluctant to comply with these orders, claiming the increased cost as an unnecessary burden on the ratepayers, which included themselves; nonetheless, from 1897 the number of nurses employed in Nenagh increased and more of them had the required training.[47]

The first of the new recruits was midwife Margaret Turner, a 27-year-old widow with five children, from Dublin.[48] Nenagh seems a long way to come from Dublin, especially as there were many maternity hospitals in Dublin but, as Julia Anne Bergin tells us, there was not enough employment in Dublin for the numbers of midwives being trained.[49] The railway line in Nenagh might have influenced her decision, as it provided her with the fastest way of travelling between the city where her children lived and the town in which she lived and worked, for all except one of the children would remain in Dublin.[50] She requested and was granted permission for her middle child, Alice Patricia, then aged 6, to live with her in her apartments in the workhouse.[51] Over the next four years the nursing staff increased to four paid nurses as well as the community of five Sisters of Mercy.[52]

The Borrisokane board of guardians did not experience anything like the same problems that Nenagh had encountered with nursing staff, possibly because the infirmary was smaller and they generally did not cater for fever patients. In 1899, the nursing staff in Borrisokane infirmary consisted of two untrained nurses, Mary Cavanagh and Kate Byrne, and two pauper nurses. The board of guardians was instructed by the LGB to employ a fully trained nurse without delay and such wards maids as were required to replace the pauper nurses.[53] By 'trained nurse' they meant a nurse who was not merely 'qualified', as in one who has obtained their qualifications from a hospital recognized by the LGB, but one who possessed the highest qualifications in medical, surgical and fever work.[54] The board, however, did not accept that a trained nurse would be any better than the two nurses they already employed who they said were as good as any nurse with six months training in a hospital.[55] They managed to avoid the issue until 1901. When the matron of the workhouse fell ill and it became apparent that she would never be capable of resuming her duties they decided to employ Margaret Kelly, a trained nurse, as the new matron, thereby solving two problems at once.[56] Between the two censuses the workforce in Borrisokane remained stable, with the only addition being the new matron. The same was not true for Nenagh.

Only one of the sisters and one of the nurses who had been present in Nenagh in 1901 were still in the workhouse in 1911: Sr Mary Vincent Reidy, who was the head nurse in 1911 and Johanna Barry née FitzGerald, who had married the workhouse porter in 1903. The individual sisters who made up the community resident in the workhouse changed at times though the overall number remained at five, not all of whom worked as nurses, while the number of lay nurses had increased to seven by 1911. Margaret Turner had left the workhouse when she married RIC constable Michael Daughton in 1902 and was working as a midwife in the town (Appendix 1).

As well as the permanent staff there were often temporary nurses employed from Cork Street Fever Hospital in Dublin or Barrington's Hospital in Limerick, when required to care for patients in the fever hospital.[57] The LGB had given Dr Minnitt the power to make these appointments when necessary, without the prior approval of the board of guardians, much to the board's annoyance and complaints about the added expense.[58] By 1900 accommodation for the growing nurse population became an issue for the board.[59] When the workhouses were constructed it was not intended that there would be many paid staff so only limited staff accommodation was provided. A temporary solution was to utilize the fever hospital when it was free of patients but that meant as soon as there was even one fever patient, the nurses living there had to move out and squeeze in where they could in the available staff apartments. This left no room for any temporary nurses so they were sometimes put up in one of the hotels in town, adding even more expense on the board.[60]

By 1909 it was decided by the LGB that there were actually too many nurses in Nenagh and the number needed to be reduced. To begin with, they did not need a full-time fever hospital nurse and instead should employ temporary nurses as required.[61] The LGB pointed out that the poor layout of the infirmary, with separate male and female sides that did not connect with each other, had created the need for extra nurses that were not warranted by the number of patients. Also, the number of patients in the infirmary had reduced considerably with some of the reform measures such as improved diets for the elderly. The majority of the patients had been elderly, long-term residents who did not require treatment for illness but who were in the workhouse due to 'debility'.[62] They had been placed in the infirmary to receive the superior diet available to invalids compared to the standard workhouse diet but when a better diet was made available to them in the main house then there was no need for them to be in the infirmary.[63]

A review of the census returns for Nenagh and Borrisokane workhouses for 1901 and 1911 shows that the number of people using the workhouses in the early twentieth century was much lower than their capacity. Nenagh could accommodate up to one thousand inmates. In 1901 there were 170 people using the main workhouse, ninety-five patients in the infirmary and eighteen in the wards for the mentally ill, which was a total of 283 inmates. By 1911 the total number of inmates had fallen to 230, with 130 people in the main workhouse, eighty-four patients in the infirmary and sixteen who were mentally ill. The largest age cohorts in Nenagh were children aged up to 10 years and adults aged between 61 and 80. Borrisokane could accommodate up to six hundred inmates. In 1901 there was a total of seventy-six inmates, half of whom were in the infirmary. There were only twenty-nine inmates in the main workhouse and eight people in the ward for the mentally ill. By 1911 the overall numbers of people using the workhouse had dropped to fifty-six inmates of whom thirty-three were using the infirmary, nineteen were resident in the main workhouse and four were living in the ward for the mentally ill. The age profile of the inmates in the main workhouse was equally distributed across the ages from 0 to 90 years, while the majority of patients in the infirmary were aged between 61 and 80.[64]

Between 1918 and 1919 the workhouse infirmaries would experience what Ida Milne refers to as 'the Local Government Boards' last great crisis' when an influenza pandemic swept through the country in three waves of illness: in March and October of 1918 and March 1919.[65] This international crisis, which claimed the lives of approximately 20,000 people in Ireland, put the workhouse infirmaries to the test, though only a fraction of those who were ill were hospitalized.[66] One of the casualties in Nenagh in October 1918 was 25-year-old Alice Patricia Turner, daughter of Margaret Daughton, who was one of six women in Nenagh district who died from influenza between October and November.[67]

By 1922, Ireland was experiencing enormous political change. On a night in June 1922, just before the outbreak of the Civil War, many houses in Nenagh were ransacked and burned, and shots were fired into the house of Margaret Daughton. Her family, as well as the families of every other demobilized RIC officer who had remained in the town, received notices to leave, which they complied with in one weekend.[68] The Daughtons escaped to Liverpool, where Margaret died just four years later in February 1926.[69] Nenagh workhouse did not escape the Civil War. The main building was completely destroyed by fire in 1923 though the infirmary was not affected and continued to function as a district hospital until a new hospital was built on the site in 1935.[70] Sister Mary Elizabeth Maxwell, who had been matron of the old infirmary, continued in that position until her retirement in 1947.[71] The county workhouses were reorganized under the new government: Nenagh infirmary became a district hospital with sixty-seven beds; Roscrea workhouse buildings became a district hospital with thirty-five beds, a county fever hospital with twenty-five beds and six cots and a sanatorium with fifty-two beds; and Thurles workhouse became the county home for the elderly with forty-four beds, as well as a maternity home for unmarried mothers.[72] Borrisokane workhouse and infirmary were closed in 1923.[73]

4. Tuberculosis, the Women's National Health Association and district nursing

In Ireland in 1882, three of the leading causes of death were old age, consumption and the febrile or zymotic diseases (small pox, measles, scarlet fever, diphtheria, whooping-cough, fever, diarrhoea and dysentery, and cholera). It was in this year that German physician and microbiologist Dr Robert Koch discovered the *tubercule bacillus*, thereby giving an ancient disease its new name 'tuberculosis' and proving that it was an infectious disease caused by a bacterium and not hereditary, as previously believed.[1] Tuberculosis was a worldwide public health issue but Ireland's cases increased disproportionately from the 1880s. By the beginning of the twentieth century Ireland had more cases per capita than England, Wales and Scotland.[2] Treatment options were limited and a cure would not be found until 1943 when *streptomycin* was discovered.[3] Sanatoria had been built in mountainous areas of Europe to offer therapies to patients that were thought to help them recover their health and included fresh air and good food.[4] Ireland's first sanatorium, the Royal National Hospital for Consumption for Ireland was built in Newcastle, Co. Wicklow, and operated from 1896 to 1963, taking patients from all over the country.[5] The disease has never been eradicated but levels in Ireland are low, with an average of 315 new cases per year.[6]

In 1900, deaths from tuberculosis in all its forms numbered 16,903, making it the leading cause of death in that year.[7] Tuberculosis can affect any part of the body but most commonly affects the lungs. This form is known as phthisis or pulmonary tuberculosis and it accounted for 10,076 of the deaths in 1900. Other common types included tuberculosis of the lymph nodes, known as 'scrofula' and tuberculous meningitis. The worst aspect of the disease was that 75 per cent of the deaths were in young people aged 15 to 45 years. There were few families that were not affected by it; indeed, many of the nurses mentioned in the previous chapters lost close family members to the disease. It made young widows of Margaret Turner when her first husband James died in 1895 and Rosaline Waterson, whose first husband John was only 21 when he died of phthisis in 1898 just a year after their marriage.[8] Bridget Boney lost her son John to the disease when he was only 19, in 1897, then in 1907 her husband John Walsh died of the same illness.[9] Bridget Hogan's eldest child, Denis, died in Dublin's Meath Hospital on 15 March 1920 of tuberculosis of the adrenals aged 27.[10]

Public concern was being expressed throughout the country, especially with regard to the rising death rates.[11] Action was required to prevent the disease and it would come in 1907 in the person of Countess Ishbel Aberdeen, wife of the lord lieutenant of Ireland from 1905 to 1915. Lady Aberdeen expressed a great love for Ireland and her people and wanted to meaningfully contribute to their welfare in some way. The high death rate from tuberculosis and high infant-mortality rates in cities such as Dublin and Belfast were the major health issues that faced her when she arrived in Ireland. She believed that by engaging women to work for these causes great improvements could be made so, to this end, she established the Women's National Health Association (WNHA).[12] The WNHA aimed to provide effective information and education on how to prevent tuberculosis, lobby government for better conditions in primary schools to help prevent the spread in this cohort, and better equip buildings for the reception of those with the disease.[13] The LGB had insisted on separate facilities for tuberculosis patients within workhouse infirmaries from 1901 and the Tuberculosis Prevention (Ireland) Act of 1908 introduced measures to reduce the spread of infection such as anti-spitting laws.[14] Lady Aberdeen believed that if the women of Ireland were taught what to do to prevent tuberculosis then change would happen.[15]

Through the WNHA she set up a travelling exhibition that toured the country showing women how to clean and ventilate their homes, feed their families nutritious food on a budget and care for a family member who had tuberculosis. In 1908, Nenagh Urban Council sent an invitation to Lady Aberdeen to bring the exhibition to the town. It felt that a visit from the exhibition was an 'urgent necessity' since the local doctors had told the board that 'consumption was very prevalent in the town'.[16] The exhibition was held from 3 to 5 July 1908, during which time a large meeting was held, at which Lady Aberdeen encouraged the establishment of a WNHA branch. There was support for this organization from all sectors of the community including the clergy, doctors and the council and interest in membership from the ladies of Nenagh and the surrounding district.[17] The newly formed association started with a committee of fourteen ladies with the following elected as officers: Mary Frances Prittie, Lady Dunalley, as president; Amy Simla Webb and Julia McMahon as vice-presidents; Mabel Dease as secretary and Grace Stawell as treasurer.

They quickly set about raising funds 'to provide a trained nurse for Nenagh and district, who will visit the sick poor in their own homes, nursing any case of illness or accident, except infectious cases', which they felt was the best way to assist in the crusade against tuberculosis.[18] This nurse would provide a service that was not currently available. She was not a replacement for any of the existing medical relief services such as the dispensary midwives, for their role was solely the care of a mother and baby through pregnancy, delivery and the month afterwards. In 1909, they were in a position to employ Mary Alice Doyle, though they continued to fundraise for the position by holding concerts, theatricals and bazaars, besides seeking general subscriptions. Doyle had spent four years training and working in the Mater Misericordiae Hospital in Dublin before completing her district nurse training in St Lawrence's Home, established in 1891 for Catholic nurses.[19] A similar home for Protestant nurses, St Patrick's Home for Nurses, had been established in 1876. Both institutions, which were in Dublin, were affiliated to Queen Victoria's Jubilee Institute for Nurses (QNI) established in 1887, and the nurses were known as 'Queen's nurses', 'Jubilee nurses' or 'district nurses'.[20] Doyle was received well, and at the third annual meeting of the WNHA Nenagh branch it was reported that 'the Queen's jubilee district nurse continued to be more highly thought of everyday'. From January to the end of September that year she had nursed 232 cases and paid 2,368 visits.[21] The WHNA nurses employed in Nenagh tended to stay for an average of about three years. In 1912, Doyle left Nenagh and was replaced by Kathleen Walsh, who held the post until 1917.[22] Mary Angela Murphy held the post from October 1917 to March 1920 and was praised for her hard work, particularly during the influenza pandemic.[23] In February 1920, Kathleen Quinn moved from Blarney to Nenagh to take up the post, leaving in August 1922 to marry William O'Brien from Ivy House, Nenagh.[24] She was replaced in September 1922 by Florence Mary Gilmartin from Templederry, who was the first of Nenagh's Jubilee nurses native to Nenagh.[25] Each of these nurses was highly qualified, with both general nursing and midwifery qualifications as well as the extra training in district nursing from St Lawrence's Home. All except Mary Alice Doyle, whose father was a sea captain, came from a farming background and all of them were single at the time they were employed in the district.[26]

The WNHA in Nenagh as elsewhere formed a subcommittee, the Nenagh Nursing Association, specifically to deal with the work and finances of the district nurse, keeping these separate to the other work of the association. It was one of 320 district nursing associations set up in Ireland.[27] Breathnach writes that funding the nurse was a universal problem throughout Ireland. Insufficient funds threatened the existence of the district nursing service in many areas. Fundraising, subscriptions and other donations were required to finance the nurse, her house and equipment required for her to carry out her job.[28] Grant funding was available from the county council under the Tubercular scheme and from the urban council under the Child and Welfare scheme, that started in Nenagh in November 1919, which together covered about half of the cost of the nurse.[29] The latter scheme added visits to mothers and their babies to the tasks that district nurses had to perform.

While Breathnach argues that district nurses faced problems in gaining acceptance in the locality, Elizabeth Prendergast paints a more positive picture of the experience.[30] District nursing was acknowledged as being the most demanding branch of nursing, requiring a woman that not only held the required qualifications of hospital training and midwifery as well as certification in district nursing but who was also 'possessed of refinement and tact' as such a lady could

> more readily introduce the necessary sanitary reforms without hurting the feelings of the poor; and when necessity demands it, herself do menial work, sweep, dust and tidy a room, take away

curtains and carpets in which infection and germs may lurk, and make it a place in which a speedy recovery is possible.[31]

Her life in the district was centred entirely on the needs of her patients: she was on call twenty-four hours a day, seven days a week, with one month's holiday leave each year. If she was fortunate enough to work in a district near another Jubilee nurse they could cover for each other on alternate Sundays, allowing each to have every second Sunday free. She was a respected member of the community and often dedicated her entire adult life to the district, remaining in one area from the time of her appointment after training until retirement or death. As we see from the example of Nenagh, however, where the nurses changed frequently, this was not always the case. She cared for the sick, carried out school inspections, attended to emergencies, was a health educator and in many instances was the only social-service provider in the community. The members of the DNA, who employed her, were also her main financial, social and emotional support. These voluntary committees were made up of hard-working, well-intentioned, wealthy, well-respected members of the community.[32] Nenagh Nursing Association operated until 1958, when they appealed to the county council to take over the work as the association could no longer continue due to insufficient funding. In consequence, north Tipperary county council decided to employ a public-health nurse for Nenagh dispensary district in 1959.[33] District nursing, domiciliary nursing and midwifery services began to amalgamate in the 1960s into the branch of nursing known as 'public-health nursing'. This was a state-funded service that removed the need for voluntary organizations such as the DNAs.[34]

The work of the nurses and the practical public-health advice she and the members of the WNHA spread had a positive effect on the death rates for the disease. In 1919, deaths from all types of tuberculosis numbered 8,643, almost half of what they had been in 1900. There was still a long way to go before tuberculosis was curable, so the campaigns to prevent it and stop its spread would continue until then. In the reorganization of the health system in the 1920s the people of north Tipperary would not have to leave the county to access a sanatorium as one was created in part of what had been Roscrea workhouse, which operated until the 1960s.[35] Tuberculosis rates had fallen to 7,000 cases a year by the 1950s and, though it has not been eradicated, in 2019 (the latest year for which figures are available) there were only 267 cases notified to the health protection surveillance centre of the health service executive.[36]

Conclusion

Nurses and midwives have been present in society and performing important functions throughout history, but these were not roles that were valued or coveted and they were left to be carried out by those who were poor, illiterate and willing to do the jobs that no-one else wanted. The transition from that low base to them becoming respectable professions, backed by scientific learning, standardized training and qualifications took almost a hundred years to complete. Legislation governing both professions passed in 1918 and 1919 could be seen as an end or a start point: the end of campaigning for a professional body of nurses and midwives or the beginning of their ongoing development.

This study has focused on how that process was supported in the poor-law unions of Borrisokane and Nenagh, spearheaded by reformers, medical doctors and members of local government. The voice of the patient is largely missing from the narrative. This unique viewpoint is underrepresented because, just as Breathnach said of handywomen, the patients did not leave their own writings. Their experience of the system was recorded only when there was a complaint or a problem. In the workhouse infirmaries and fever hospital there was a definite benefit to patients in being cared for by employed staff, with or without qualifications, rather than reluctant or disinterested pauper inmates. As seen in the case of the nuns in Nenagh infirmary before they gained nursing qualifications, however, and the nurses in Borrisokane infirmary who were said to be the equal of any qualified nurse, if patient care was good then there was no cause for complaint or desire for change. Where care was poor or neglectful, the patients or, more often, their relatives made complaints that contributed to changes being made.

The patient's voice was more evident when it came to midwifery, however, as pregnant women chose who they wanted to deliver their babies. Even those who were entitled to free care from the dispensary midwives could choose an alternative birth attendant if they wanted.

Qualified and unqualified midwives coexisted for much of the period covered in this study, though this was not always an amicable arrangement as the experience of Mary Anne Nolan in Portroe attests. Any animosity expressed by the 'handywomen' towards their trained counterparts was understandable considering their livelihoods were threatened by the growing numbers of qualified midwives. They were also heading to a time when their practice became illegal unless they could afford to register. The shift towards hospital deliveries would see the end of their practice except in very remote areas of the country. Though the birth registers are a limited source, they give some evidence of the choices women made for their confinements. This is a resource that could be explored further.

Nursing and midwifery became better paid for those who had qualifications and training but it was still a low-paid job with the nurses having to haggle for increases. They benefited hugely from the foundation of the Irish Nurses Union in 1919 as they now had an organization that could advocate for them for better pay and conditions, especially after the sharp rise in the cost of living after the Great War (1914–18). Now called the Irish Nurses and Midwives Organization (INMO), this union celebrated its centenary in 2019 and continues to support nurses and midwives in Ireland.

The creation of the Irish Free State resulted in some changes to the old systems of health provision, though these were not dramatic and mostly consisted of reorganizing the functions of the workhouse infirmaries and renaming the governance structures. The dispensary system was untouched until 1970 when the Health Boards were formed.[1] The nurses who had been employed under the old system would continue doing the same duties under the new system. It was a base from which the modern healthcare system grew. It would never go back to a time when it was deemed appropriate for a person without the specific education and qualifications to perform the duties of nurses and midwives. The nursing associations that funded the district nurse would continue to do so until the state began financing public-health nursing throughout the country. This lack of change in the job itself, as opposed to the organization controlling it, shows that nursing and midwifery were important essential services within the health system.

A notable observation that would be worth exploring further is the familial link associated with nursing and midwifery, suggesting that these professions 'ran in the family'. Of the nurses and midwives identified for this study and named in the appendices, there were four family groups including the Lyons sisters, Johanna and Annie, both of whom became dispensary midwives; the FitzGerald sisters, Johanna and Kathleen, who were nurses in Nenagh infirmary; Mary Ellen Toohey and her aunt Rosaline Waterson who were both midwives; and mother and daughter, Anne and Mary McDonald, who were dispensary midwives in Toomevara. A fifth family group were mother and daughter district midwives in Borrisokane, Helen Kelly and Mary Aherne, though Mary was still a child during the time frame of the study and did not become the district midwife until after her mother's retirement in 1947.

A limitation of this study is the deliberate and considered omission of the contribution of nurses and volunteers during the Great War. While this subject did fall within the timeframe of the study, due to other constraints this area could not be fully explored. In short, young women left Borrisokane and Nenagh unions to nurse wounded soldiers both at the front and at military hospitals in Britain and Ireland. Many more women of all ages stayed at home and joined the War Hospital Supply Depots, making bandages and garments, knitting socks and collecting sphagnum moss for bandages.[2] This is another area for future study.

The present study has explored and illuminated the contribution of nurses and midwives regardless of their title or educational attainment in health provision in north Tipperary from 1882 to 1922. Without directly accessing the voices of these women, this work has sought to discover them and take account of their unique contribution to health provision. Such an exploration has generated valuable evidence on this previously unexamined area.

Appendix 1

Name	Birthplace	Occupation 1901	Occupation 1911	Other
Ellen Bennett/ Helen Kelly	Co. Tipperary	Nurse (Borrisokane and Terryglass district midwife)	Nurse (Borrisokane district midwife)	Farmer's daughter 1901 Living with her parents, siblings and children in Rathcabbin 1911 Living with her husband and children in Borrisokane
Mary Bergin	King's County	Not found	Nurse	1911 Living in O'Meara's Hotel, Nenagh
Bridget Boney/ Bridget Walsh	Co. Tipperary	Nurse midwife	No occupation recorded (Still practising midwifery in 1919 as per birth registers)	Farmer's daughter 1901 Living alone in Graces Street, Nenagh 1911 Living with two boarders
Marguerite Bowles	Co. Cork	Hospital nurse	Trained nurse	1901 Employed privately by William Reilly Minchin in Kilbarron 1911 in Hume Street Hospital, Dublin
Janet Bianca Bruce	King's County	Not found	Landowner and farmer	Army major's daughter 1911 Living with sister in Coolbawn Awarded Royal Red Cross Medal for setting up military hospitals in Belfast in 1915
Kate Byrne	Co. Tipperary	Infirmary nurse	Nurse	1901 and 1911 Borrisokane Workhouse Infirmary Katherine Byrne, aged 65 years, died 1917
Mary Cavanagh	Co. Tipperary	Infirmary nurse	Nurse	Farmer's daughter 1901 and 1911 Borrisokane Workhouse Infirmary Retired in 1913 due to ill health after 22 years' service.

(*Sources*: 1901 and 1911 censuses, with additional information from registers for births, deaths and marriages, newspapers and other documents)[1]

Name	Birthplace	Occupation 1901	Occupation 1911	Other
Florence Harriet Cole (Sr Mary Magdalen)	England	Sister of Mercy	Sister of Mercy	1901 Nenagh Workhouse Infirmary 1911 Living with community in Birr
Teresa Daly (Sr Margaret)	King's County	Sister of Mercy	Sister of Mercy	1901 Nenagh Workhouse Infirmary 1911 Living with community in Birr
Mary Anne Dancer/ Mary Anne Nolan	Nenagh, Co. Tipperary	Servant	Portroe district midwife (based in Ballina)	Labourer's daughter 1901 Living with her mother Ellen Kelly in Hanley's Lane, Nenagh 1911 Living with husband Thomas Nolan and mother Ellen Kelly in Ballina
Katherine (Kathleen) Diver	Co. Donegal	Nurse	Not found	1901 Visiting in Rathmines, Dublin on night of census 1902 Resigned from post as Cloughjordan dispensary midwife to go to South Africa
Mary Alice Doyle	Co. Down	Not found – was training in Mater Hospital at this time	District Queen's nurse	Sea Captain's daughter 1911 Living in Summerhill, Nenagh
Helena FitzGerald	Co. Limerick	Sister of Mercy	N/A	1901 Nenagh Workhouse Infirmary Died in Birr in 1908 of pneumonia
Johanna FitzGerald/ Johanna Barry	Co. Tipperary	Nurse	Infirmary nurse	Farmer's daughter 1901 and 1911 Nenagh Workhouse Infirmary Her husband is John Barry, workhouse porter
Catherine/ Kathleen FitzGerald	Co. Tipperary	Scholar	Infirmary nurse	Farmer's daughter 1901 living with parents and siblings in Clonmel 1911 Nenagh Workhouse Infirmary, living with her sister Johanna Barry, brother-in-law and their family
Kathleen Garrett	Co. Mayo	Not found	Maternity nurse	1911 With Revd Griffin's family in Lorrha who have week-old baby

Name	Birthplace	Occupation 1901	Occupation 1911	Other
Alice Gleeson	Co. Tipperary	Nurse	No occupation recorded	1901 Nenagh Workhouse Infirmary 1911 Living with cousins in Nenagh Died of cardiac failure on 3 June 1911 aged 78 years
Ellen Gleeson	Co. Tipperary	Nurse	Midwife	1901 Living with son and daughter-in-law 1911 Living alone in Garrykennedy
Mary Gleeson	Co. Tipperary	Sister of Mercy	Sister of Mercy	1901 Nenagh Workhouse Infirmary 1911 Living with community in Gaol Street, Nenagh
Mary Gleeson	Co. Tipperary	Not found	Nurse	1911 Nenagh Workhouse Infirmary
Catherine Growney	Co. Meath	Not found	Hospital nurse	1911 Working in private house (Saunders family, Borrisokane)
Susan Gunson	Co. Tipperary	Scholar	Hospital nurse	Farmer's daughter 1911 Living with parents and siblings in Greenhall
Norah Harty	Co. Tipperary	Not found	Nurse	1911 Nenagh Workhouse infirmary
Kate Heffernan née Kelly	Co. Tipperary	Not found – family moved about a lot; husband a gardener	Maternity nurse	Farmer's daughter 1911 Living in Terryglass with her 5 children. Husband Jeremiah died of cancer in 1910
Marie Hickey	Co. Tipperary	Nurse	No occupation recorded	Mason's daughter 1901 and 1911 Living with husband and children in Silver Street, Nenagh
Bridget Hogan	Co. Tipperary	No occupation recorded	Nurse (Cloughjordan district midwife)	Farmer's daughter 1901 Living in Tipperary town with her husband (a newsagent and tobacconist) and their 3 children) 1911 Living in Main Street, Cloughjordan with one son in the house on night of census
Margaret Kennedy	Co. Tipperary	Not found	Trained nurse (matron of workhouse)	1911 Borrisokane Workhouse Infirmary
Norah Kennedy	Co. Tipperary	Not found	Trained nurse (night nurse)	1911 Borrisokane Workhouse Infirmary

Name	Birthplace	Occupation 1901	Occupation 1911	Other
Annie Kinnane	Co. Tipperary	Not found	Sister of Mercy nurse	1911 Nenagh Workhouse Infirmary
Kate Kyte	Co. Tipperary	Housekeeper/ farmer's daughter	Nurse (Portroe district midwife)	1901 Living with parents and siblings in Silvermines 1911 Living alone in Portroe
Annie McDonald/ McDonnell	Co. Tipperary	Midwife (Toomevara district midwife)	Midwife (Toomevara district midwife)	Servant's daughter 1901 and 1911 Living in Toomevara with her children
Lily McDowell	Co. Tipperary	Hospital nurse	Not found	Daughter of R.I.C. Sergeant 1901 Living with widowed mother (post mistress) and siblings in Carney
Kathleen McKeogh	Co. Tipperary	Not found	Nurse	Farmer's daughter 1901 Not at home 1911 Living with widowed mother and siblings in Ballina
Mary Agnes Maher	Co. Tipperary	Midwifery nurse (Silvermines district midwife)	Nurse (Silvermines district midwife)	Farmer's daughter 1914 Married Thomas McSoley
Elizabeth G. Manly	Co. Tipperary	Not found	Hospital nurse	Farmer's daughter 1901 Not at home 1911 Living with her siblings in Derrycastle
Sarah Mann	King's County	Nurse	Hospital nurse	Farmer's daughter 1901 Living with or visiting her sister (Teresa Courtney) and her family in Knigh, Nenagh 1911 Visiting in Monkstown, Cork
Anna Maria Maxwell (Sr Mary Elizabeth)	Co. Westmeath	Not found	Unpaid nurse	1911 Nenagh Workhouse Infirmary Matron of Infirmary Matron of county hospital 1935–45. Died in 1969 aged 91 years
Catherine Moore	Co. Tipperary	Midwife	No occupation recorded	Labourer's daughter 1901 Living with 3 of her adult children in Abbey Lane, Nenagh 1911 Living alone
Kate O'Brien	Co. Fermanagh	Nurse	Not found	1901 Nenagh Workhouse Infirmary

Name	Birthplace	Occupation 1901	Occupation 1911	Other
Ellen O'Connor	Cork	Not found	Trained nurse	1911 In O'Meara's Hotel, Nenagh
Norah O'Leary	Co. Tipperary	Not found	Nurse	1911 Nenagh Workhouse Infirmary
Norah Quin	Limerick	Hospital nurse	Not found	1901 Employed privately by Biggs family, Bellevue, Kilbarron
Josephine B. (Johanna) Reidy	Nenagh, Co. Tipperary	Farmer's daughter	Pupil midwife, Rotunda Hospital, Dublin	1901 Lived in Carrigatogher with her mother and brother Appointed as district midwife, Portroe, 1912
Mary Teresa Reidy (Sr Mary Vincent)	Co. Tipperary	Sister of Mercy	Sister of Mercy Head nurse	1901 and 1911 Nenagh Workhouse Infirmary Died 1 Dec. 1915 aged 58 years
Mary Rea (Sr Columba)	Co. Limerick	Sister of Mercy	Sister of Mercy Nurse	1901 Member of community in Peter Street, Nenagh 1911 Nenagh Workhouse Infirmary 1915 Appointed matron of the workhouse
Teresa Scanlan	Co. Sligo	Not found	Nurse	1911 Nenagh Workhouse Infirmary
Annie Seymour	Co. Tipperary	Farmer's daughter	Nurse	1901 Living with parents and siblings in Knigh 1911 Nenagh Workhouse Infirmary
Susan Stanley	Co. Tipperary	Hospital nurse	Not found	1901 Employed in private house in Riverstown
Lillian Hamilton Taylor	Co. Tipperary	Scholar/ farmer's daughter	Hospital nurse	1901 and 1911 Living with widowed mother and sibling in Carney Commons
Margaret Frances Turner/ Margaret Frances Daughton	Dublin	Nurse	Professional nurse	Engine driver's daughter 1901 Nenagh Workhouse Infirmary 1911 Living with husband and children in Barrack Street, Nenagh
Rosie/ Roseline Waterson	Co. Meath	Midwife	Nurse (Nenagh district midwife)	Labourer's daughter 1901 Living in Co. Kildare 1911 Living in dispensary in Summerhill, Nenagh in 1911
Katherine M. Whealey	Co. Tipperary	Domestic servant Rotunda Hospital	District nurse Newport	Farmer's daughter from Rathnaleen, Nenagh. Midwifery certificate from National Maternity Hospital, Dublin

Appendix 2

Name	Birthplace	Occupation 1901	Occupation 1911	Other
Julia Hough	Co. Tipperary	Scholar	Cook – domestic servant	Army pensioner's daughter 1901 Living with parents and siblings in Newlawn, Terryglass 1911 Working for Esmonde family of Drominagh Demesne Married Kieran Dalton in 1912 Nurse Dalton from 1920 Appointed district midwife Shinrone, Co. Offaly
Johanna M. /Josie Lyons	Co. Tipperary	Scholar	No occupation recorded	Farmer's daughter 1901 and 1911 Living with parents and siblings in Kilmastulla, Birdhill Appointed district midwife to Terryglass in September 1911
Anna M./ Annie Lyons	Co. Tipperary	Scholar	No occupation recorded	Farmer's daughter 1901 and 1911 Living with parents and siblings in Kilmastulla, Birdhill Appointed Nenagh dispensary midwife in 1919
May McDonald/ Mary McDonnell	Co. Tipperary	Scholar	No occupation recorded	Printer's daughter 1901 and 1911 Living with widowed mother (midwife) and siblings 1914 Appointed Toomevara dispensary midwife on her mother's retirement

(*Sources*: 1901 and 1911 censuses, with additional information from registers for births, deaths and marriages, newspapers and other documents)[2]

Name	Birthplace	Occupation 1901	Occupation 1911	Other
Bridget Rohan/ Bridget Tompkins	Co. Tipperary	Dressmaker	Dressmaker	Shopkeeper's daughter 1901 Living with sister, brother, visitor and 4 boarders (including her future husband) in Barrack Street, Nenagh 1911 Living with sister and two boarders Nurse Tompkins from *c.*1918
Sarah Teehan	Co. Roscommon	Not found	No occupation recorded	RIC pensioner's daughter 1911 Living with widowed father and sister in Main Street, Cloughjordan Working as independent midwife in Cloughjordan area from *c.*1917

Appendix 3

WOMEN WHO ATTENDED AT LEAST TWO BIRTHS OR WERE IDENTIFIED
AS 'NURSE' IN NENAGH AND BORRISOKANE UNIONS AS PER BIRTH
REGISTERS FOR 1870, 1875, 1882, 1896, 1906 AND 1919[3]

Name	Address	Mentioned in birth register years	Other
Mary Allen	Toomevara	1870	Record states 'nurse present at birth'
Mary Akins	Spout Road, Nenagh	1870	Records state 'nurse in attendance' Nenagh dispensary nurse from 1842 Advertised in *Nenagh Guardian* in 1859 as a 'licensed accoucheur and ladies' nurse-tender'
Ellen Bennett/ Helen Kelly (*née* Reddan)	Rathmore, Borrisokane	1906, 1919	Dispensary midwife, Borrisokane and Terryglass *c.*1900–10, then Borrisokane only until 1947; set up private nursing home in Borrisokane
Bridget Boney/ Bridget Walsh	Graces Street, Nenagh	1896, 1906, 1919	Records state 'nurse present at birth' Bridget Walsh, Graces Street, Nenagh, widow, nurse, died 5 Apr. 1930 aged 77 of pernicious anaemia, myocarditis and heart failure
Bridget Brennan	Lorrha	1896	Record states 'present at birth' Bridget Brennan, nurse-teacher, widow, died 31 Mar. 1899 aged 75 years of bronchitis
Margaret Brown	Borrisokane	1870	Records state 'nurse present at birth'
Josephine B. Carey (*née* Reidy)	Portroe	1919	Dispensary midwife, Portroe, 1912–19
Elizabeth de Clare	Summerhill, Nenagh	1906	Provided cover for dispensary midwives
Judy Commins	Portroe	1870	Records state 'present at birth and in attendance'
Margaret Daughton (*née* Carroll)	Barrack Street and Summerhill, Nenagh	1906, 1919	Records state 'present at birth' Previously Margaret Turner, nurse in Nenagh infirmary

Name	Address	Mentioned in birth register years	Other
Margaret Dudley	Borrisokane	1870	Records state 'nurse present at birth'
Bridget Feeney	Desborough, Nenagh	1875	Records state 'nurse present at birth'
Mary Fogarty	Old Turnpike, Nenagh	1882	Record states 'nurse present at birth'
Catherine/Kate Grace	Pound Street, Nenagh	1882, 1896	Record states 'nurse present at birth'
Mary Green	Bownes Lane, Silver Street and Abbey Lane, Nenagh	1870, 1875, 1882	Records state 'nurse in attendance', 'nurse present at birth'
Marie Hickey (*née* McDonnell)	Silver Street, Nenagh	1906	Record states 'present at birth'
Mary Hickey	Kilcommon, Nenagh	1896	Record states 'present at birth'
Anne Hogan	William Street, Nenagh	1875, 1882	Records state 'nurse present at birth'
Judy Hough	Borrisokane	1882	Records state 'nurse present at birth' Not found on 1901 census Judy Haugh, spinster, domestic servant, died 17 Apr. 1905 in Borrisokane workhouse aged 80 years of senile decay
Bridget Hogan (*née* McCormack)	Cloughjordan	1911	Cloughjordan district midwife, 1902–20 Died by drowning in river in Nov. 1920 aged 57
Winifred Hogan	Abbey Lane, Nenagh	1896, 1906	
Anne Keef/ Annie Keeffe	High Street, Newport	1870, 1875, 1882	Records state 'present at birth' Anne Keef of High Street, Newport, labourer's widow, died at home on 30 Mar. 1885 aged 85
Margaret Kennedy	Borrisokane	1870	Record states 'nurse present at birth'
Mary Kennedy	Lisheen, Rathcabbin	1882	Record states 'present at birth'
Mary Kennedy	Eglish	1882	Record states 'present at birth'

Name	Address	Mentioned in birth register years	Other
Mary Kemple	Kildarby, Borrisokane	1870, 1882	Records state 'nurse present at birth'
Kate Kyte	Newport	1919	Dispensary midwife, Portroe, 1911–12 Dispensary midwife, Newport from 1912
Annie Lyons	Summerhill, Nenagh	1919	Dispensary midwife, Nenagh and Knigh, 1919–47 Nurse Gill from 1925
Mary Maher/ Mary McSoley	Silvermines	1906, 1919	Dispensary midwife, Silvermines from 1900 to 1947
Mary Mangan	Newport	1896	Not found on 1901 census Mary Mangan, midwife, widow, formerly of Newport, died in Nenagh workhouse 12 Oct. 1902 aged 55 years of liver disease
Mary Meara	Firmount, Terryglass	1875	Records state 'present at birth'
Catherine Moore (*née* Quigley)	Spout Road, Nenagh	1875, 1882, 1896, 1906	Records state 'nurse present at birth' Catherine Moore, Dublin Road, Nenagh, widow, maternity nurse, died 8 Mar. 1926 aged 81 years of senile decay and cardiac failure
Mary McCormack	Curragh, Castletown	1870	Records state 'present at birth and in attendance'
Anne McDonald (*née* Dargan)	Toomevara	1896, 1906	Dispensary midwife, Toomevara 1894–1914 Anne McDonald, widow, retired midwife, died 29 Aug. 1934 aged 85 years of senile decay and cardiac failure
Catherine McLoughlin	Graces Street, Nenagh	1875, 1882	Records state 'nurse present at birth' Advertised in *Nenagh Guardian* in 1865 as 'Ladies' nurse tender' with diploma to practise midwifery from Rotunda Lying-in hospital
Ellen Nolan	Garrykennedy	1870	Record states 'present at birth and in attendance'
Margaret O'Brien	Birr Road and Turnpike, Nenagh	1870, 1875, 1882, 1896	Records state 'nurse present at birth', 'nurse in attendance' Not found in 1901 census Margaret O'Brien, Graces Street, Nenagh, widow, midwife, died 11 Aug. 1909 aged 85 years of general debility and cardiac failure

Name	Address	Mentioned in birth register years	Other
Mary O'Donohue (*née* McDonald)	Toomevara	1919	Dispensary midwife, Toomevara, 1914–47
Biddy Ryan	Borrisokane	1870, 1875, 1882	Records state 'nurse present at birth' Bridget Ryan, widow, nurse, died in Borrisokane workhouse 24 Nov. 1893 aged 82 years of debility (for 4 years)
Winifred Ryan	Roscrea	1919	Records state 'nurse present at birth'
Betty Stanley	Borrisokane	1870	Record states 'nurse present at birth'
Sarah Teehan	Cloughjordan	1919	Record states 'nurse present at birth' Private midwife, provided cover for dispensary midwives
Bridget Tompkins (*née* Rohan)	Silver Street, Nenagh	1919	Private midwife who provided cover for dispensary midwives from 1918; set up Nurse Tomkins' Nursing Home, later St Mary's Nursing Home, Kenyon Street, Nenagh in 1930
Mary Ellen Toohey (*née* McCormack)	Turnpike, Nenagh	1919	Provided cover for dispensary midwives including Rosaline Waterson, her aunt.
Mary Walsh	Ballycahane, Silvermines	1870	Records state 'present at birth'
Rosaline Waterson (*née* McCormack)	Summerhill, Nenagh	1906	Dispensary midwife, Nenagh and Knigh 1902–19 Rosaleen McCarthy, Toomevara, married, wife of farmer, died in St John's Hospital, Limerick on 13 Jan. 1931 aged 54 years of acute obstruction (2 days) and cardiac failure
Rachel Watson	Cornagluck, Ballyquirk, Lorrha	1906	Record states 'present at birth' 1911 census, labourer's wife, no occupation recorded, aged 35 years
Kate Whealey	Newport	1906	Dispensary midwife, Newport 1904–12

Notes

ABBREVIATIONS

DNA   District Nursing Association
HC   House of Commons
INMO   Irish Nurses and Midwives Organization
LGB   Local Government Board
QNI   Queen Victoria's Jubilee Institute for Nurses
RIC   Royal Irish Constabulary
WNHA   Women's National Health Association

INTRODUCTION

1 Maria Luddy, 'District nursing in Ireland, 1815–1974', *Tipperary Historical Journal* (1996), p. 164.

2 Gerard Fealy, *A history of apprentice nurse training in Ireland* (London, 2006), pp 7–10.

3 Margaret Preston, 'The good nurse: women philanthropists and the evolution of nursing in nineteenth-century Dublin', *New Hibernia Review/Iris Éireannach Nua*, 2:1 (1998), pp 95–6.

4 John O'Sullivan, 'Two hundred years of midwifery, 1806–2006', *Ulster Medical Journal*, 75:3 (2006), pp 213–17.

5 Frances Carruthers and Martin Duffy, *The viceregal microbe: politics and the battle against tuberculosis in Ireland* (Leicester, 2018), p. 57.

6 Laurence Geary, *Medicine and charity in Ireland, 1718–1851* (Dublin, 2004), pp 18–20.

7 *Public medical relief: Royal commission for inquiring into the condition of the poorer classes in Ireland: Appendix B*, p. 1 [369], HC 1835, xxxii, pt 2, 2.

8 *Survey of hospital archives in Ireland* (National Archives, 2015), p. 63.

9 Geary, *Medicine and charity in Ireland*, pp 54–69.

10 Pigot and Co. Directory 1824 and Slaters Directory of Munster 1846 available at www.failteromhat.com, last accessed 28 July 2020; Slaters Directory of Ireland 1856 available at www.igp-web.com, last accessed 28 July 2020; *Nenagh Guardian*, 18 June 1859; ibid., 17 June 1865; ibid., 17 June 1871.

11 *Public medical relief: royal commission for inquiring into the condition of the poorer classes in Ireland: Appendix B*, p. 1 [369], HC 1835, xxxii, pt 2, 89–97.

12 Geary, *Medicine and charity in Ireland*, pp 54–69.

13 Ibid., pp 40–53.

14 Ibid., pp 70–92.

15 Daniel Grace, 'The cholera outbreak of 1832–33 in Co. Tipperary', *Tipperary Historical Journal* (2011), pp 39–67.

16 *Public medical relief: Royal commission for inquiring into the condition of the poorer classes in Ireland: Appendix B*, p.1 [369], HC 1835, xxxii, pt 2, Supplement 149–51.

17 Nenagh Workhouse and Fever Hospital available at www.dia.ie, last accessed 4 July 2020; *Nenagh Guardian*, 8 Dec. 1849.

18 *Nenagh News*, 22 July 1899.

19 [1 and 2 Vict., c. lvi] *An act for the more effectual relief of the destitute poor in Ireland* (1838); [12 and 13 Vict., c. civ] *An act to amend the acts for the more effectual relief of the destitute poor in Ireland* (1849).

20 [14 and 15 Vict., c. lxviii] *An act to provide for the better distribution, support and management of medical charities in Ireland; and to amend an act of the eleventh year of her majesty, to provide for the execution of the laws for the relief of the poor in Ireland*

(1851); [25 and 26 Vict., c. lxxxiii] *An act to remedy the laws in force for the relief of the destitute poor in Ireland, and to continue the powers of the commissioners* (1862).

21 Poor Relief (Ireland) Act, 1862; Fealy, *Apprentice nurse training in Ireland* (2006), pp 7–10; *An act to remedy the more serious defects in the existing law relating to the relief of the poor and certain other matters of local government and for that purpose to amend temporarily the laws relating to the matter aforesaid*, No. 9 (1923).

22 Poor Relief (Ireland) Act, 1838; Griffith's valuation available at www.nli.ie, last accessed 4 July 2020.

23 Geary, *Medicine and charity in Ireland*, pp 95–122.

24 *The history and working of the Irish poor-law medical system* (London, 1870), pp 1–16.

25 Fealy, *Apprentice nurse training in Ireland*, pp 7–10.

26 *The Irish poor-law medical system* (1870), p. 14.

27 Ibid., pp 2–16.

28 Maria Luddy, *Women and philanthropy in nineteenth-century Ireland* (Cambridge, 1995), p. 49; Fealy, *Apprentice nurse training in Ireland*, pp 13–14.

29 Fealy, *Apprentice nurse training in Ireland*, pp 13–14.

30 *Nenagh Guardian,* 8 July 1882.

31 Luddy, *Women and philanthropy*, p. 51.

32 Fealy, *Apprentice nurse training in Ireland*, p. 11; 'Workhouse reform in Ireland. Conference in Dublin', *The British Medical Journal*, 2:1867 (1896), pp 1048–9.

33 *Commissioners for administering laws for relief of poor in Ireland: fifteenth annual report with appendices*, p. 535, [C. 2966], HC 1862, xxiv, 17.

34 Rita Walsh, 'Borrisokane Workhouse', *Tipperary Historical Journal* (2007), p. 59; Daniel Grace, *The Great Famine in Nenagh poor-law union, Co. Tipperary* (Nenagh, 2000), p. 19.

35 *Local Government Board for Ireland: eleventh report with appendices*, p.1, [C. 3681], HC 1883, xxix, 285–6.

36 *Local Government Board for Ireland: fifteenth report*, p.1, [C. 5124], HC 1887, xxxvii, 207–8; *Annual report of the Local Government Board for Ireland, for year 1911–12*, p. 1 [Cd. 6339], HC 1913, xxxvii, 325; W.E. Vaughan and A.J. FitzPatrick

(eds), *Irish Historical Statistics, Population 1821–1971* (Dublin, 1978), p. 10.

37 *Local Government Board for Ireland: eleventh report with appendices*, p. 1 [C. 3681], HC 1883, xxix, 285–6.

38 Ibid.

39 *Nenagh News*, 16 Jan. 1915.

40 *Public medical relief: Royal commission for inquiring into the condition of the poorer classes in Ireland: Appendix B*, p.1 [369], HC 1835, xxxii, pt 2, Supplement 90–3.

41 *Commissioners for administering laws for relief of poor in Ireland under Medical Charities Act: first annual report*, p. 325 [1609] HC 1852–3, l, 129–31; Historic maps for Lorrha and Carrigahorig, 1837–42 and 1888–1913 available at www.osi.ie, last accessed 15 Aug. 2020.

42 Historic maps for Portroe and Ballina 1888–1913 available at www.osi.ie, last accessed 15 Aug. 2020.

43 *Nenagh Guardian*, 15 May 1897.

44 *Commissioners for administering laws for relief of poor in Ireland: fifteenth annual report with appendices*, p. 535 [2966], HC 1862, xxiv, 17.

45 Ibid., p. 18.

46 *Nenagh Guardian*, 21 June 1902; ibid., 13 Aug. 1902; ibid., 7 May 1910.

47 Poor Relief (Ireland) Act, 1838.

48 Nenagh Workhouse available at www.dia.ie, last accessed 4 July 2020.

49 Walsh, 'Borrisokane Workhouse', p. 59.

50 Poor Relief (Ireland) Act, 1838.

51 [59 and 60 Vict., c. vi]. *An act to enable women to be elected and act as poor-law guardians in Ireland* (1896).

52 *Nenagh News*, 29 Apr. 1905.

53 [35 and 36 Vict., c. l]. *An Act for constituting a Local Government Board in Ireland, and vesting therein certain functions of the Lord Lieutenant, the Privy Council, and the Chief Secretary to the Lord Lieutenant, concerning the Public Health and Local Government, together with the powers and duties of the Commissioners for administering the Laws for the Relief of the Poor in Ireland* (1872).

54 Ibid.

55 *Local Government Board for Ireland: twenty-sixth annual report with appendices*, p. 1, [C. 8958], HC 1898, xli, 67–8.

56 Liam Kennedy and Leslie Clarkson, 'Birth, death and exile: Irish population

history, 1700–1921' in B.J. Graham and
L.J. Proudfoot (eds), *A historical geography
of Ireland* (London, 1993), pp 158–64.

57 W.E. Vaughan and A.J. FitzPatrick (eds),
Irish historical statistics, population 1821–1971
(Dublin, 1978), p. 10.

58 *Commissioners for administering laws for relief
of the poor in Ireland: sixth annual report with
appendices,* p. 159, [1645], HC 1852–3,
l, 113–16; *Local Government Board for
Ireland: tenth report with appendix,* p. 1 [C.
3311] HC 1882, xxxi, 89.

59 *Commissioners for administering laws for relief
of the poor in Ireland: twenty-third annual
report with appendix,* p.1 [C. 156], HC
1870, xxxvi, 162.

60 *Nenagh Guardian,* 5 June 1880; ibid., 13
Oct. 1897.

61 Ibid., 8 July 1882.

62 Ibid.

63 'Irish workhouse infirmary reform', *The
British Medical Journal,* 2:1867 (1896), pp
1059–60.

64 *Nenagh Guardian,* 8 July 1882.

65 Ibid., 13 Nov. 1897.

66 Ibid., 14 Sept. 1898; *Nenagh News,* 23
Feb. 1901.

67 *Thirty-seventh detailed annual report of the
registrar-general of marriages, birth and deaths
in Ireland, 1901* [Cd. 697], HC 1900, pp
1–20.

68 History of tuberculosis available at
www.cdc.gov, last accessed 2 July 2020.

69 *Nenagh Guardian,* 8 July 1908.

70 Ibid., 19 Jan. 1901.

71 Ibid., 1 July 1908.

72 Ibid., 19 Jan. 1901.

73 Ibid., 16 Dec. 1905.

74 Ibid., 1 July 1908.

75 *Roll of Queen's Nurses,* 16 (1909–10), p. 115.

76 Kevin McKenna, Catherine Clune
Mulvaney and Catherine O'Neill,
'Nursing then, nursing now', *World of
Irish Nursing and Midwifery,* 28:6 (2020),
pp 18–19.

77 Fealy, *Apprentice nurse training in Ireland,*
p. xii.

78 *Nenagh Guardian,* 10 Apr. 1982.

I. PROFESSIONAL NURSING AND MIDWIFERY
IN NENAGH AND BORRISOKANE POOR-LAW
UNIONS

1   Census returns 1901 and 1911 for the
occupation of 'nurse' available at www.
census.nationalarchives.ie, last accessed
13 Sept. 2019; *Nenagh Guardian,* 8 Oct.
1918.

2   Fealy, *Apprentice nurse training in Ireland,*
p. 152.

3   Luddy, *Tipperary Historical Journal,* p. 164.

4   Brian Abel-Smith, *A history of the nursing
profession* (London, 1960), p. 60 as quoted
in Fealy, *Apprentice nurse training in
Ireland,* p. 17.

5   Ciara Breathnach, 'Handywomen and
birthing in rural Ireland, 1851–1955',
Gender and History, 28:1 (2016), pp 34–56;
Julia Anne Bergin, 'Birth and death in
nineteenth-century Dublin's lying-in
hospitals' in Elaine Farrell (ed.), *'She said
she was in the family way': pregnancy and
infancy in modern Ireland* (London, 2012),
p. 99.

6   Bergin, *Pregnancy and infancy in modern
Ireland* (2012), p. 91.

7   Anne Summer, 'The mysterious demise
of Sarah Gamp: the domiciliary nurse
and her detractors, c.1830–1860',
Victorian Studies, 32:3 (1989), p. 385.

8   'The central midwives board', *The British
Medical Journal,* 1:2319 (1905), p. 1294.

9   Fealy, *Apprentice nurse training in Ireland*
(2006), p. 39; J. Power, 'Proposed
midwives act for Ireland', *The British
Medical Journal,* 2:2907 (1916), pp 408–9.

10 Preston, *New Hibernia Review/Iris
Éireannach Nua* (1998), pp 91–110.

11 Fealy, *Apprentice nurse training in Ireland,*
p. 152.

12 Preston, *New Hibernia Review/Iris
Éireannach Nua* (1998), pp 91–110;
Summer, *Victorian Studies* (1989),
p. 365.

13 McKenna, Clune Mulvaney and O'Neill,
World of Irish nursing and midwifery,
pp 18–19.

14 Fealy, *Apprentice nurse training in Ireland,*
p. 2; Preston, *New Hibernia Review/Iris
Éireannach Nua* (1998), pp 91–110.

15 Preston, *New Hibernia Review/Iris
Éireannach Nua* (1998), p. 102.

16 Hylda Beckett, 'St Vincent's Hospital,
Dublin 1834–1984', *Dublin Historical
Record,* 37:3/4 (1984), pp 137–43; History
of the Sisters of Mercy available at
www.mercyworld.org, last accessed 8
Apr. 2020.

17 Caitríona Clear, *Nuns in nineteenth-century Ireland* (Dublin, 1987), p. 57.

18 Summer, *Victorian studies* (1989), pp 376–8.

19 J. Power and L. Kidd, 'Proposed midwives act for Ireland', *The British Medical Journal*, 2:2907 (1916), pp 408–9; Breathnach, *Gender and history* (2016), pp 34–56.

20 Charles Dickens, *The life and adventures of Martin Chuzzlewit* (Boston, 1872), pp 187–483.

21 E.A. Bent, 'The education and practice of midwives in the 20th century' in V.R. Bennett and L.K. Brown (eds), *Myles Textbook for Midwives* (11th ed., 1989), p. 691.

22 Summer, *Victorian studies* (1989), pp 365–86.

23 Judith Moore, *A zeal for responsibility: the struggle for professional nursing in Victorian England, 1868–1883* (Georgia, 1988) quoted in Preston, *New Hibernia Review/Iris Éireannach Nua* (1998), p. 109.

24 Summer, *Victorian Studies* (1989), p. 382.

25 Breathnach, *Gender and history* (2016), pp 34–56; Moore, *A zeal for responsibility* (1988), quoted in Preston, *New Hibernia Review/Iris Éireannach Nua* (1998), p. 109.

26 Bent, *Myles textbook for midwives* (1989), p. 694.

27 *Census of Ireland 1891: Area, population and number of houses: Occupations, religion and education volume II, Provence of Munster*; p. 1 [C. 6567, 6567–I, 6567–II, 6567–III, 6567–IV, 6567–V, 6567–VI, 5657–VII, 6567–VIII, 6567–IX], HC 1892, xci, 787; Vaughan and FitzPatrick (eds), *Irish historical statistics* (1978), p. 10.

28 Vaughan and FitzPatrick (eds), *Irish historical statistics* (1978), p. 10.

29 Census of Ireland 1901 and 1911, population of Co. Tipperary, occupation 'nurse' available at www.census.national archives.ie, last accessed 24 Jan. 2020.

30 Ibid.

31 Return for Nenagh workhouse staff 190 available at www.census.nationalarchives.ie, last accessed 16 Aug. 2020.

32 Birth registers Nenagh district available at www.irishgenealogy.ie, last accessed 3 Aug. 2020.

33 Marriage record for Mary Maher and Thomas McSoley 1914 available at www.irishgenealogy.ie, last accessed 10 Aug. 2020.

34 Preston, *New Hibernia Review/Iris Éireannach Nua* (1998), pp 91–110.

35 *Nenagh Guardian*, 2 Dec. 1854; ibid., 13 Apr. 1878; ibid., 2 Feb. 1880.

2. HANDYWOMEN, MIDWIVES AND THE DISPENSARY SYSTEM

1 Bent, *Myles' textbook for midwives* (1989), p. 692.

2 Breathnach, *Gender and History* (2016), pp 34–56.

3 Bent, *Myles' textbook for midwives* (1989), p. 693.

4 Power and Kidd, *The British Medical Journal* (1916), pp 408–9.

5 *Nineteenth detailed annual report of the registrar-general of marriages, births and deaths in Ireland, 1882* [C. 3795], HC 1883, 5–18.

6 *Nenagh Guardian*, 20 Jan. 1841.

7 Ibid., 18 Aug. 1841.

8 Ibid., 21 Jan. 1843; ibid., 8 Feb. 1845.

9 Ibid., 12 Mar. 1851; *Commissioners for administering laws for relief of poor in Ireland under Medical Charities Act : first annual report*, p .325 [1609], HC 1852–3, l, 129–31.

10 Birth record Nenagh district 1870 available at www.irishgenealogy.ie, last accessed 11 Aug. 2020.

11 *Nenagh Guardian*, 17 June 1865.

12 Birth registers Nenagh district 1875 and 1882 available at www.irishgenealogy.ie, last accessed 9 Aug. 2020.

13 *Nenagh Guardian*, 17 June 1871.

14 Ibid., 11 May 1842.

15 [26 and 27 Vict., c. xi] *An Act for the Registration of Births and Deaths in Ireland* (1863).

16 Death record for Margaret O'Brien 1909 available at www.irishgenealogy.ie, last accessed 12 Aug. 2020.

17 *Nenagh Guardian*, 20 Jan. 1869.

18 Ibid., 20 Jan. 1869.

19 Ibid., 3 Mar. 1877.

20 Ibid., 21 Nov. 1877.

21 *Local Government Board for Ireland: eleventh report with appendices*, p. 1 [C. 3681], HC 1883, xxix, 287.

22 *Annual report of the Local Government Board for Ireland, for the year 1912–13*, p. 457 [Cd. 6978], HC 1913, xxxii, 325.

23 *Commissioners for administering laws for relief of poor in Ireland: fifteenth annual report with appendices*, p. 535 [C. 2966], HC 1862, xxiv, 15; William Thomson, 'The Irish poor-law medical service', *The British Medical Journal*, 50:1833 (1896), p. 391.

24 *Commissioners for administering laws for relief of poor in Ireland under Medical Charities Act: first annual report*, p. 325 [1609], HC 1852–3, l, 47.

25 Bergin, *'She said she was in the family way': pregnancy and infancy in modern Ireland*, p. 106.

26 Annual Reports of the Local Government Board for Ireland available at www.archive.org, last accessed 28 Aug. 2020.

27 *Commissioners for administering laws for relief of poor in Ireland: fifteenth annual report with appendices*, p.535 [C. 2966], HC 1862, xxiv, 17.

28 *Thirty-first annual report of the Local Government Board for Ireland, for the year ending 31st March 1903*, p.1 [Cd. 2012], HC 1904, xxvii, xvi.

29 Ibid.

30 *Nenagh Guardian*, 17 Oct. 1914.

31 Ibid., 15 Aug. 1914.

32 Ibid.

33 *Nenagh News*, 7 July 1906.

34 *Nenagh Guardian*, 11 Oct. 1919.

35 *Nenagh News*, 23 June 1906.

36 Ibid., 4 Sept. 1897; *Nenagh Guardian*, 26 Oct. 1898.

37 *Nenagh Guardian*, 23 July 1902.

38 Death record for Mary Mangan 1902 available at www.irishgenealogy.ie, last accessed 8 Aug. 2020.

39 Death record for Judy Haugh 1905 available at www.irishgenealogy.ie, last accessed 12 Aug. 2020; Death record for Anne Keef 1885 available at www. civilrecords.irishgenealogy.ie, last accessed 12 Aug. 2020.

40 Ibid., 20 Aug. 1904.

41 *Nenagh Guardian*, 8 Feb. 1913; ibid., 22 May 1926.

42 *Nenagh News*, 4 Sept. 1897.

43 Ibid., 20 Aug. 1904.

44 Census record 1901 available at www. census.nationalarchives.ie, last accessed 17 Aug. 2020; *Nenagh News*, 1 Mar. 1919.

45 *Nenagh News*, 8 Aug. 1908.

46 Ibid., 20 Aug. 1904.

47 Ibid., 19 Aug. 1911.

48 *Nenagh Guardian*, 28 Sept. 1946.

49 Ibid., 6 Oct. 1945.

50 Census record 1901 available at www. census.nationalarchives.ie, last accessed 17 Aug. 2020.

51 *Nenagh Guardian*, 5 Apr. 1947.

52 Ibid., 12 July 1947.

53 Ibid., 17 Mar. 1906.

54 Ibid., 10 Feb. 1906.

55 *Nenagh News*, 26 Nov. 1910.

56 Ibid., 30 July 1910.

57 *Nenagh Guardian*, 25 Nov. 1882; ibid., 17 Aug. 1907.

58 *The Nationalist*, 25 Aug. 1915.

59 *Nenagh News*, 15 Sept. 1917; ibid., 30 Mar. 1918.

60 Ibid., 26 May 1917.

61 Ibid., 3 July 1920.

62 Ibid., 27 Jan. 1906.

63 Ibid., 8 Aug. 1908.

64 *Thirty-eighth detailed annual report of the registrar-general of marriages, births and deaths in Ireland 1901* [Cd. 1225], HC 1902, 1–18; *Forty-third detailed annual report of the registrar-general of marriages, births and deaths in Ireland 1906* [Cd. 3663], HC 1907, v–xxxi; *Forty-eighth detailed annual report of the registrar-general of marriages, births and deaths in Ireland 1911* [Cd. 6312], HC 1912, v–xxxv; *Fifty-third detailed annual report of the registrar-general of marriages, births and deaths in Ireland 1916* [Cd. 8647], HC 1917, v–xxv; *Fifty-eighth detailed annual report of the registrar-general of marriages, births and deaths in Ireland 1921* (1922), v–xix.

65 *Nenagh Guardian*, 28 Sept. 1946.

3. NUNS, NURSES AND THE WORKHOUSE

1   Michael Francis Cox, 'Nursing in Irish poor-law hospitals', *The British Medical Journal*, 2:2129 (1901), pp 1184–5.

2   Laurence Geary, 'The medical profession, healthcare and the poor law in nineteenth-century Ireland' in Virginia Crossman and Peter Gray (eds), *Poverty and welfare in Ireland, 1838–1948* (Dublin, 2011), pp 189–206.

3   Annual Reports of the Local Government Board for Ireland available at www.archive.org, last accessed 28 Aug. 2020.

4 Folk medicine in the School's collection (1937–8) available at www.duchas.ie, last accessed 18 Aug. 2020.

5 Helen Burke, *The people and the poor law in 19th-century Ireland* (Dublin, 1987), pp 262–72.

6 Fealy, *Apprentice nurse training in Ireland*, p. 12.

7 Jeremiah Dowling, *The Irish poor law and the poor house* (Dublin, 1872), p. 86.

8 Virginia Crossman, *Poverty and the poor law in Ireland* (Liverpool, 2014).

9 *Nenagh Guardian*, 29 Oct. 1864.

10 Ibid., 28 July 1877; ibid., 10 July 1880.

11 Ibid., 5 June 1880; ibid., 5 Feb. 1881.

12 *Nenagh Guardian*, 5 Feb. 1881.

13 Ibid., 2 Apr. 1881.

14 Ibid., 30 Apr. 1881.

15 Fealy, *Apprentice nurse training in Ireland*, p. 12; *Nenagh News*, 20 Jan. 1900.

16 O'Brien, *Sisters of Mercy*, pp 84–91; *Nenagh Guardian*, 10 Apr. 1982.

17 *Nenagh Guardian*, 10 Apr. 1982.

18 Ibid., 8 July 1882.

19 O'Brien, *Sisters of Mercy*, pp 84–91; *Nenagh Guardian*, 29 July 1882.

20 O'Brien, *Sisters of Mercy*, pp 84–91.

21 Clear, *Nuns in nineteenth-century Ireland*, p. 59; *Nenagh News*, 10 Mar. 1900.

22 *Nenagh Guardian*, 23 July 1881.

23 Ibid., 1 Mar. 1919.

24 Ibid., 8 Aug. 1888.

25 Ibid., 13 Dec. 1890.

26 *Nenagh News*, 17 Aug. 1895.

27 Ibid., 21 Sept. 1895.

28 *Nenagh Guardian*, 28 Oct. 1893.

29 Ibid., 8 June 1895.

30 Death record for Michael Reynolds available at www.irishgenealogy.ie, last accessed 3 June 2020.

31 *Nenagh News*, 13 July 1895.

32 Ibid., 31 Aug. 1895.

33 *Nenagh News*, 28 Sept. 1895.

34 Death record for Alice Cahalan available at www.irishgenealogy.ie, last accessed 3 June 2020.

35 Death record for Margaret Flannery available at www.irishgenealogy.ie, last accessed 3 June 2020.

36 *Nenagh News*, 1 Aug. 1896.

37 *Nenagh Guardian*, 14 Aug. 1897.

38 *Nenagh News*, 25 Sept. 1897; *Nenagh Guardian*, 4 Feb. 1899.

39 *Nenagh News*, 20 Jan. 1900.

40 *Nenagh Guardian*, 14 Aug. 1886.

41 *Nenagh News*, 31 Aug. 1895.

42 *Nenagh Guardian*, 1 Dec. 1894.

43 Ibid., 7 Oct. 1882.

44 'Pauper nurses', *The British Medical Journal*, 2:1906 (1897), p. 104.

45 'Irish workhouse infirmary reform', *The British Medical Journal*, 2:1867 (1896), pp 1059–60; ibid., 1860 (1896), pp 471–2.

46 Virginia Crossman, *Poverty and the poor law in Ireland* (2014).

47 *Nenagh News*, 1 June 1907.

48 Birth, death and marriage registers for south Dublin 1887–95 available at www.irishgenealogy.ie, last accessed 20 May 2020.

49 Bergin, *Pregnancy and infancy in modern Ireland* (2012), pp 91–111.

50 Turner children census 1901 available at www.census.nationalarchives.ie, last accessed 24 Aug. 2020.

51 *Nenagh News*, 17 Apr. 1897.

52 Census returns for Nenagh workhouse staff 1901 and 1911 available at www.census.nationalarchives.ie, last accessed 24 Aug. 2020.

53 *Nenagh News*, 22 July 1899.

54 Ibid., 29 June 1907.

55 *Nenagh Guardian*, 19 May 1900.

56 *Nenagh News*, 23 Feb. 1901.

57 *Nenagh Guardian*, 24 Feb. 1900.

58 Ibid., 6 Oct. 1900.

59 *Nenagh News*, 14 Apr. 1900.

60 *Nenagh Guardian*, 29 Sept. 1900.

61 *Nenagh News*, 1 May 1909.

62 *Nenagh News*, 20 Jan. 1900.

63 Nenagh Guardian, 9 Sept. 1908.

64 Census returns for Nenagh and Borrisokane workhouses 1901 and 1911 available at www.census.national archives.ie, last accessed 21 July 2019.

65 Ida Milne, 'Influenza: the Irish local governments boards last great crisis' in Donnacha Seán Lucey and Virginia Crossman (eds), *Healthcare in Ireland and Britain from 1850: voluntary, regional and comparative perspectives* (2014), pp 217–36.

66 Ibid., p. 219.

67 Death record for Alice Turner available at www.irishgenealogy.ie, last accessed 19 Aug. 2020.

68 *Irish Independent*, 13 June 1922.

69 *The Nationalist*, 13 Feb. 1926.

70 *Nenagh Guardian*, 23 Nov. 1935.

71 Ibid., 22 Nov. 1969.

72 Ibid., 28 Sept. 1947.

73 Walsh, *Tipperary Historical Journal* (2007), p. 68.

4. TUBERCULOSIS, THE WOMEN'S NATIONAL HEALTH ASSOCIATION AND DISTRICT NURSING

1   Dr Robert Koch available at www. nobelprize.org, last accessed 20 Apr. 2020.

2   'The vital statistics of Ireland', *The British Medical Journal*, 1:2246, 1904, pp 157–8.

3   John Frith, 'History of tuberculosis', *Journal of Military and Veterans' Health*, 22:2 (2014), p. 39.

4   Ibid., p. 37.

5   Royal National Hospital for Consumption for Ireland catalogue of documents held by Royal College of Physicians of Ireland available at www. iar.ie, last accessed 25 Mar. 2022.

6   Tuberculosis in Ireland in 2018 available at www.hpsc.ie, last accessed 11 Jan. 2021.

7   *Thirty-seventh detailed annual report of the registrar-general of marriages, births and deaths in Ireland 1900* [Cd. 697], HC 1901, 1–20.

8   Death record for James Turner available at www.irishgenealogy.ie, last accessed 19 Aug. 2020; death record for John Waterson 1898 available at www.irish genealogy.ie, last accessed 19 Aug. 2020.

9   Death record for John Boney 1897 available at www.irishgenealogy.ie, last accessed 19 Aug. 2020; death record for John Walsh 1907 available at www. irishgenealogy.ie, last accessed 19 Aug. 2020.

10 Death record for Denis Hogan 1920 available at www.irishgenealogy.ie, last accessed 19 Aug. 2020.

11 *Irish Daily Independent*, 6 Dec. 1901.

12 Maureen Keane, *Ishbel, Lady Aberdeen in Ireland* (Dublin, 1999), p. 15.

13 *Sláinte, Journal of the Women's National Health Association*, Issues 1–12 (1909).

14 [5 Edw. 7] *An Act to prevent the spread and provide for the treatment of Tuberculosis: and for the other purposes connected therewith* (1908).

15 *Nenagh Guardian*, 8 July 1908.

16 Ibid., 6 June 1908.

17 Ibid., 8 July 1908.

18 Ibid., 26 Aug. 1908.

19 *Roll of Queen's Nurses*, 16 (1909–10), p. 115.

20 Ciara Breathnach, '"…it would be preposterous to bring a Protestant here": religion, provincial politics and district nurses in Ireland, 1890–1904' in Donnacha Seán Lucey and Virginia Crossman (eds), *Healthcare in Ireland and Britain from 1850: voluntary, regional and comparative perspectives* (2014), pp 161–80.

21 *Nenagh Guardian*, 25 Nov. 1911.

22 *Roll of Queen's Nurses*, 16 (1909–10), p. 119.

23 Ibid., 21 (1914–15), p. 263; *Nenagh Guardian*, 2 Nov. 1918.

24 *Roll of Queen's Nurses*, 24 (1918–9), p. 160; *Nenagh News*, 2 Sept. 1922.

25 Ibid., 22 (1915–16), p. 102; *Nenagh Guardian*, 11 Nov. 1922.

26 *Roll of Queen's Nurses*, 16, 21 and 24.

27 Elizabeth Prendergast, 'Jubilee Nurses', *Dublin Historical Record*, 66:1/2 (2013), pp 59–66.

28 Breathnach, *Healthcare in Ireland and Britain* (2013), pp 161–80.

29 *Nenagh Guardian*, 15 Jan. 1921.

30 Breathnach, *Healthcare in Ireland and Britain* (2013), pp 161–80; Prendergast, *Dublin Historical Record* (2013), pp 59–66.

31 'District Nursing', *The Nursing Record,* 5 Apr. 1888, p. 10.

32 Prendergast, *Dublin Historical Record* (2013), pp 59–66.

33 *Nenagh Guardian*, 19 Dec. 1959.

34 National Council for the Professional Development of Nursing and Midwifery, *Agenda for the future professional development of public health nursing* (2005), p. 9.

35 Operating costs of St Cronan's sanatorium Roscrea, 1952–1964, Dáil Éireann debate, Thursday, 25 June 1964 available at www.oireachtas.ie, last accessed 27 Aug. 2020.

36 Tuberculosis in Ireland in 2020 available at www.hspc.ie, last accessed 27 Aug. 2020.

CONCLUSION

1   *An act to amend and extend the Health Acts, 1947 and 1966, and certain other enactments, to provide for the establishment of bodies for the administration of the Health Services, and for other matters connected with the matters aforesaid* (1970).

2 Nurses and volunteers during WWI available at www.redcross.org.uk, last accessed 28 Aug. 2020.

APPENDICES

1 Census returns 1901 and 1911 for the occupation of 'nurse' in Lower Ormond available at www.census.nationalarchives.ie, last accessed 13 Sept. 2019; Registers of births, deaths and marriages available at www.irishgenealogy.ie, last accessed 20 Apr. 2020.

2 Census returns 1901 and 1911 for the occupation of 'nurse' in Lower Ormond available at www.census.nationalarchives.ie, last accessed 13 Sept. 2019; Registers of births, deaths and marriages available at www.irishgenealogy.ie, last accessed 20 Apr. 2020.

3 Birth, marriage and death registers available at www.civilrecords.irishgenealogy.ie, last accessed 1 May 2020.